ENGLISH GRAMMAR

100 Tragically Common Mistakes*

and How to Correct Them

Sean Williams

ZEPHYROS PRESS

Copyright © 2019 by Zephyros Press, Emeryville, California

No part of this publication may be reproduced, stored in a retrieval system, or transmitted in any form or by any means, electronic, mechanical, photocopying, recording, scanning, or otherwise, except as permitted under Sections 107 or 108 of the 1976 United States Copyright Act, without the prior written permission of the Publisher. Requests to the Publisher for permission should be addressed to the Permissions Department, Zephyros Press, 6005 Shellmound Street, Suite 175, Emeryville, CA 94608.

Limit of Liability/Disclaimer of Warranty: The Publisher and the author make no representations or warranties with respect to the accuracy or completeness of the contents of this work and specifically disclaim all warranties, including without limitation warranties of fitness for a particular purpose. No warranty may be created or extended by sales or promotional materials. The advice and strategies contained herein may not be suitable for every situation. This work is sold with the understanding that the Publisher is not engaged in rendering medical, legal, or other professional advice or services. If professional assistance is required, the services of a competent professional person should be sought. Neither the Publisher nor the author shall be liable for damages arising herefrom. The fact that an individual, organization, or website is referred to in this work as a citation and/or potential source of further information does not mean that the author or the Publisher endorses the information the individual, organization, or website may provide or recommendations they/it may make. Further, readers should be aware that websites listed in this work may have changed or disappeared between when this work was written and when it is read.

For general information on our other products and services or to obtain technical support, please contact our Customer Care Department within the United States at (866) 744-2665, or outside the United States at (510) 253-0500.

Zephyros Press publishes its books in a variety of electronic and print formats. Some content that appears in print may not be available in electronic books, and vice versa.

TRADEMARKS: Zephyros Press and the Zephyros Press logo are trademarks or registered trademarks of Callisto Media Inc. and/or its affiliates, in the United States and other countries, and may not be used without written permission. All other trademarks are the property of their respective owners. Zephyros Press is not associated with any product or vendor mentioned in this book.

Interior and Cover Designer: Will Mack
Art Producer: Karen Beard
Editor: Justin Hartung
Production Editor: Andrew Yackira
Illustrations: Will Mack

Author Photo © Morgan Black

ISBN: Print 978-1-64152-373-8 | eBook 978-1-64152-374-5

This book is dedicated to those who love the English language, who appreciate its dynamic flexibility, and who understand that its rules are not always set in stone.

Contents

Introduction x

{ CHAPTER ONE }

Grammar Goofs 1

1. Incomplete Sentences 2
2. Gone and Went 3
3. Phrasal Verbs 4
4. Who/Whom 5
5. Compound Relative Pronouns 6
6. Nominative/Objective/ Possessive Pronouns 8
7. To/Too/Two 10
8. Affect/Effect 11
9. Ending a Sentence with a Preposition 13
10. Starting a Sentence with a Conjunction 14
11. Misplaced Modifiers 16
12. Dangling Modifiers 18
13. Possessive Pronouns with Gerunds 19
14. Dual Possession 21
15. Double Genitive 22
16. Subjunctive Mood I: If I Were . . . 24
17. Subjunctive Mood II: I Demand That . . . 25
18. May and Might 26
19. Get, Got, and Gotten 28
20. Indefinite Pronouns: Each 30
21. Helping Verbs: To Have 31
22. Helping Verbs: To Be 32
23. Helping Verbs: To Do 33
24. Reflexive Pronouns: Myself 35
25. Double Negatives 36

{ CHAPTER TWO }

Punctuation Saves Lives 39

26. Comma Usage 40
27. Comma Splice 42
28. Apostrophes for Pluralization 43
29. Hyphens 44
30. Capitalization 46
31. Quotation Marks 47
32. Em Dash and En Dash 48
33. Ellipses 50
34. Missing Accent Marks 51
35. Semicolons 52
36. Possessives with Names Ending in S 54
37. Ending a Declarative Sentence with a Question Mark 55
38. Colons 56
39. The Vocative Comma 57
40. Pride Capitals 59
41. Scare Quotes 60
42. Punctuation for Currency 62
43. Apostrophes for Holidays 63
44. Run-On Sentences 64
45. Double Spaces After a Period 66

{ CHAPTER THREE }

Word to the Wise 69

46. Sex vs. Gender 70
47. Weather vs. Climate 71
48. Like vs. Such As 72
49. Irregardless 74
50. Set vs. Sit 75
51. Lay vs. Lie 76
52. Unique 78
53. Will vs. Shall 79
54. Than vs. Then 81
55. Less vs. Fewer 82

56. Loose vs. Lose 83
57. Literally 84
58. Number and Amount 85
59. Could of/Should of/ Would of 87
60. A Lot vs. Alot 88
61. Weather vs. Whether vs. Wether 89
62. Breath vs. Breathe 90
63. Comprise 92
64. Everyday vs. Every Day 93
65. There/They're/Their 94
66. Etc. vs. Ext. 96
67. Historic/Historical 97
68. Between vs. Among 98
69. That/Which/Who 100
70. Its and It's 101
71. Whose and Who's 102
72. Your and You're 103
73. i.e. and e.g. 105
74. A While and Awhile 106

{ CHAPTER FOUR }

High Style 109

75. Order of Adjectives 110
76. Further vs. Farther 111
77. Accept vs. Except 112
78. Redundancies 114
79. Clichés 116
80. Jargon 118
81. Singular "They" 120
82. Differences Between American English and British English 122
83. Contranyms 123
84. Gendered Professions 124
85. Religions and Their Adherents 126
86. Writing Numbers 127
87. "Verbing" and "Nouning" 129
88. Comparatives 130
89. Superlatives 131
90. Feel Good vs. Feel Well 133

91. Parallel Structure 134

92. Better Than He/Him 136

93. Active Voice vs. Passive Voice 137

94. Number Agreement 139

95. Orient, Orientate, and Oriental 141

96. Among/Amongst and While/Whilst 142

97. Discourse Markers 144

98. Demonstratives 145

99. Split Infinitives 146

100. Indeterminate Personal Pronoun Usage 147

Parts of Speech Cheat Sheet 150

Punctuation Cheat Sheet 152

50 Substitutions for Long-Winded Phrases 155

Glossary 160

Resources 166

{ INTRODUCTION }

Everyone Makes Misstakes

I once made a mistake in another language that made the national news. I had been living in West Java (a province of Indonesia) to study music, and I went to a music party at the provincial governor's house. Most people were sitting on the floor, as was the norm. I was leaning against a wall near the musicians so I could study what they were doing; I was also trying to be as inconspicuous as a redheaded white girl could be in Southeast Asia. The governor invited me to sit in a chair, as a foreign guest, but I politely declined, telling him in my allegedly fluent Indonesian that I would rather lean against the wall . . . or so I thought. In fact, I told him and everyone around me that I would prefer to cry out! The two words that I used were separated by a single letter: *bersandar* vs. *bersangar*. I can still hear not only their raucous laughter ringing in my ears, but also my mistake repeated over and over. If only there hadn't been a reporter in the room!

English has so many words that are separated by a single letter. If you have ever struggled with *effect* and *affect*, *further* and *farther*, or *than* and *then*, I can assure you that you are in great company. This book is your secret decoder ring: a quick and easy reference tool that will help you remember everything from whether to double the consonant in the past tense of *cancel* (spoiler: don't) to knowing the difference between *who* and *whom*.

I wrote this book because I am not just a college professor; I am also a friend, colleague, mom, and person who wants all English speakers to be able to speak and write with clarity and confidence. Inside this book, you'll find 100 of the most common mistakes in grammar, punctuation, vocabulary, and style. My goal is for you to be (metaphorically, at least) running toward clarity, rather than running from murkiness. Leave your tragic mistakes behind and, with apologies to William Shakespeare, let slip the dogs of grammar!

{ CHAPTER ONE }

Grammar Goofs

Most of us learned proper grammar when we were young. But, over the years, mistakes turn into bad habits, which turn into fodder for mockery from the grammar sticklers in our lives. These errors are among the most common you'll find.

1. Incomplete Sentences

It's important to remember: "When a sentence is incomplete." Um, what? When a sentence is incomplete, no one knows what you're talking about. A half-finished sentence makes for a half-baked thought.

INCORRECT

- Whether the stolen shirt was in her purse.
- As if they hadn't flirted already!
- No way he could eat any more.

CORRECT

Most incomplete sentences are linked to a sentence either before or after the incomplete phrase in question. Adding "The security guard wanted to see" to "whether the stolen shirt was in her purse" transforms an incomplete sentence about a stolen shirt into a perfectly understandable complete sentence.

MEMORY TIP

Every complete sentence needs a subject—the person, place, thing, or idea that is doing or being something—and a predicate (which finishes an idea about the subject).

2. Gone and Went

Go is one of the 200 or so irregular verbs that can make English-language learners tear out their hair. It's simple enough to use "I go" or "he goes" correctly, but mastering the various tenses can be a struggle for even native English speakers.

INCORRECT

- We've *went* to work every day this year.
- Their cousin *gone* home.
- My granddad said that he *gone* fishing.

CORRECT

The irregular verb *to go* uses simple past tense—*went*—to indicate something that may still be happening. Where is he? He *went* to the store. (Maybe he's still there!) When you include a variant of the auxiliary verb *to have,* it changes into the perfect tense. Using *have* means the action is complete: Their cousin *has gone* home. (He isn't returning!) You never *have went* anywhere, though.

MEMORY TIP

Consider these sentences: "I *went* shopping" and "She *went* to school." Are they permanent? They are not. At some point she'll be coming home from school. No one writes a sad country song titled "She Went"; they all say that "she's gone." In the words of the late country singer Troy Gentry's song "Gone," when someone *has gone,* they are "like all the good things that ain't never comin' back." Note that last phrase; it's over.

3. Phrasal Verbs

You use phrasal verbs all the time! Many are made up of two-word phrases with a verb and a preposition (*try out*) and some contain three words (*look forward to*). Even though they're very common, it's still easy to make a mistake when using them in a sentence.

INCORRECT

- We sat down with the bagels and *divided up them.*
- I'm looking forward to *see* you soon.

CORRECT

The two most common errors are misplaced pronouns (as in *divided up them*), and neglecting to use an –ing verb in a three-word phrase. Keep the constituent parts of a phrasal verb together so that you *divide up* the bagels. In the common three-word phrases, don't forget the –ing at the end of the verb. I'm looking forward to *seeing* you soon.

MORE TO KNOW

Some three-word phrasal verbs are transitive and need a noun to be complete. You can *get away with* murder, *look down on* hoi polloi, and *take care of* your aging relative.

4. Who/Whom

People seem to be terrified of *whom*, and for good reason. Most of us never learned how to use *whom* because—and this is a secret—our teachers didn't understand it either. Fret no more! You may now use *whom* with confidence.

INCORRECT

- *Whom* does this belong to?
- Ask not for *who* the bell tolls.
- Let me know *whom* said that; I can't remember *whom* it was.

CORRECT

The heart of the matter is whether the word is the subject or object of the sentence. When you're working with the subject, use who. *Who* said it? She said it! (As the subject of the sentence, you could also use her name instead of *who*. Hana said it!) If the word in question is the object of the sentence, use whom. This belongs to *whom*? It belongs to him.

MEMORY TIP

Wondering if you've used the correct word? If you can replace the word with "he" or "she," the proper choice is *who*. If the replacement can be "her" or "him," *whom* is the correct usage.

QUIZ

What order should *who* and *whom* appear in the following sentences?

> ______ says I don't know grammar? _____ should I mark up with my red pen?

He/she = who (subject), so "*who* says" is correct. Him/her = whom (object), so "*whom* should I" is correct. "*He* says" and "I should mark *him* up" answer the questions.

5. Compound Relative Pronouns

The next time a teenager rolls their eyes at you, says "Whatever!" and stomps away, lure them back with your grammatical brilliance by saying, "Oh, honey! You just correctly used a *compound relative pronoun*!" So many people are confused by this concept, but it's easy to use the proper word.

INCORRECT

- Go with those people, *whichever* they are headed.
- Did you tell them *whoever* you are?

CORRECT

Whatever, whichever, wherever, whoever, and *whomever* are all compound relative pronouns. They join one clause to another, as in "*Whatever* candy you choose, I won't be angry," "Go with those people, *wherever* they are headed," and "You may dance with *whomever* you wish." These pronouns are inherently open and inviting of various options, which is, after all, what we all want in life.

MORE TO KNOW

As pronouns, these words serve subjects or objects: "*Whoever* [subject] left their dishes on the table needs to return and clean up." "I will go with *whomever* [object]." They are compounds because they add *-ever* to what, who, and other such question words: "*Whatever* do you want at this hour?" They also act as conjunctions because they join phrases: "I will eat *whatever* you're eating."

6. Nominative/Objective/ Possessive Pronouns

This common mistake is especially tricky when there are two pronouns. Once you learn how to use the proper pronoun, you'll hear mistakes all around you. Luckily, there's an easy trick to ensure you've chosen the right word.

INCORRECT

- Bring that to him and *I.*
- *She* cats don't belong to *my.*

CORRECT

The difficulty most often arises with more than one object pronoun. "Bring that to *him* and *me*" is right; many people will incorrectly say "*him* and *I*." "I visited *him* and *her*" is correct, while "I visited *he* and *she*" is incorrect. To get it right every time, remove one of the two pronouns: "Bring that to *him*" (correct) and "Bring that to *I*" (incorrect). That second one sounds so wrong that you will correct yourself automatically: "Bring that to *him* and *me*."

MORE TO KNOW

Personal pronouns take three different forms: nominative (I), objective (me), and possessive (both my and mine, all mine). *I* am eating this chocolate (*I* am the subject). The chocolate belongs to *me* (the object is *me*). It is *mine* (a self-sufficient possessive pronoun). The subject pronouns include *I, you, he, she, it, we, you,* and *they*. Object pronouns include *me, you, him, her, it, us, you,* and *them*. Possessive pronouns include the dependent category of *my, your, his, her, its, our, your,* and *their*; they each take an object, as in my dog. The independent category includes *mine, yours, his, hers, its, ours, yours,* and *theirs*. Notice that none of the possessive pronouns use apostrophes.

QUIZ

Which pronouns would you use, and in what order?

> _____ sat there with _____; _____ didn't realize that this table was _____.

Choose your favorite pronouns from the lists above! [Subject pronoun] sat there with [object pronoun]; [plural subject pronoun] didn't realize that this table was [possessive pronoun]. For example, *I* sat there with *him*; *we* didn't realize that this table was *hers*.

7. To/Too/Two

The main reason we confuse these three words is because they are homophones. They sound the same, so our overloaded minds mash them together into one word: *to*. It makes grammarians want to scream—two times!

INCORRECT

- You're *to* funny.
- We were going *two* buy some more popcorn today.
- They like cake so they bought *too* of them.

CORRECT

Everyone uses these words correctly in speech because they sound the same. The preposition *to* is used to indicate that one is moving "for the purpose of" or "in the direction of." We were going *to* buy some popcorn; my cat is going *to* the window. *Too* means "in excess" or "also." I ate *too* many cookies this year and he did, *too*.

FUN FACT

Anything involving *two* uses *tw* somewhere in the word: between, twice, twins, twenty, intertwine, and more.

8. Affect/Effect

Of all the word pairs separated by a single vowel, this pair is the worst for native speakers and language learners alike. Between the two words, there are four different meanings: *Affect* is both a verb (to influence) and a noun (emotional expression), and *effect* is both a verb (to make happen) and a noun (impact).

INCORRECT

- Ooh, I love those sound *affects*.
- Their son didn't consider whether eating that much candy might *effect* him.
- It is time for us all to *affect* change in our own lives.

CORRECT

About 80 percent of the time, you can trust that *affect* is a verb. "Eating a lot of candy might *affect* you. It *affected* me greatly." Similarly, *effect* is usually a noun. If you love a particular sound *effect* such as a cowbell, that *effect* is a single item—a noun (a cowbell, in this case). An *effect* is an impact: "Wow! That cowbell had quite the *effect* on the audience!"

MORE TO KNOW

In spite of the tempting rule that *affect* = verb and *effect* = noun, there are exceptions. *Affect* is also a noun, and *effect* is also a verb. *Affect* (noun) is used in psychology, and refers to emotional display. People with "flat affect" appear emotionless, even if they aren't. To *effect* (verb) is to bring about or make happen. You, too, can *effect* change in your life.

QUIZ

In what order should you use *affect* and *effect* in the following sentence?

> The beautiful lighting _____ in the clinic _____ ed the patients greatly; they made me wish to _____ changes in our policy because our own patients show little _____ at all.

Lighting *effects* can *affect* patients. To *effect* a change might change a person's *affect*.

9. Ending a Sentence with a Preposition

The rules of grammar are a lot to keep track *of*, especially when you hear that prepositions are something you're never supposed to end a sentence *with*. The cold, hard truth is that we do end sentences with prepositions in casual speech, in most written material, and in our minds.

(ALLEGEDLY) INCORRECT

- I need to hang my coat *up*; which closet can I put it *in*?
- She sure has a lot to be grateful *for*.
- Who was he talking *to*?

CORRECT

Language evolves and speech affects the way people write, so some rules fade. If you are writing for a straight-edge grammarian, tuck those prepositions inside a sentence, as in "I need to hang *up* my coat," "She has much *for* which to be grateful," and "We wondered *to* whom you were talking." Otherwise, let those prepositions fly.

FUN FACT

Winston Churchill was famously alleged to have joked, "Ending a sentence with a preposition is something up with which I will not put." It has appeared in many variants, and is attributed to dozens of people (and character types), but it's a joke about a pedantic rule that has little bearing on real life. You may let it go, dear reader, and be in good company.

10. Starting a Sentence with a Conjunction

People are often shocked to learn that most of the time it's fine to start a sentence with a conjunction. *And* it works much better if the sentence is closely related to the previous one. The main question is whether the sentence is clear and complete.

INCORRECT

- I'm staying here. *And* what was life like when you were a kid?
- *But* let me tell you: I have a long story about that.
- *Or* we could go out for drinks.

CORRECT

The sentences in the first example appear unrelated; starting the second sentence with *and* makes it seem as if it's supposed to follow naturally. *But* it doesn't. In the second example, the speaker starts a story with *but*. It's awkward, unless the speaker is using *but* to interrupt a thought and launch a different one. In the third example, *or* has no prior sentence, so the reader doesn't know the alternative.

MORE TO KNOW

Starting sentences with conjunctions, particularly when they refer to a previous sentence, is not a problem. You're on solid ground with either "I thought I liked him, but he was a jerk," or "I thought I liked him. *But* he was a jerk." The choice is really one of tone or style. *And* you can correct those who try to correct you. Don't start a paragraph with a conjunction, though.

11. Misplaced Modifiers

Misplacing your modifier can result in unexpected and startling mistakes, such as the humorous line from Groucho Marx: "I shot an elephant in my pajamas." These can be hard to spot because you know what you were trying to say, even if nobody else does!

INCORRECT

- She handed him the ice cream, *sweating from the marathon.*
- He searched all over for his *ancient daughter's toy.*

CORRECT

A modifier calls attention to something or someone. In the corrected sentence "Sweating from the marathon, she handed him the ice cream," the correct placement of the phrase "sweating from the marathon" lets you know that it describes the woman (rather than the ice cream). A *misplaced* modifier directs attention to the wrong place in a sentence, as in "He drove his dog to day care, *prepared for the faculty meeting.*" No dog is prepared for what goes on at faculty meetings. It should be: "*Prepared for the faculty meeting,* he drove his dog to day care."

FUN FACT

Decades ago, many people learned to diagram sentences, a technique that visually shows the grammatical structure of a sentence. It was a clear way to learn that a modifier has to be right next to the thing it modifies. If she drove her dog to doggie day care wearing nothing but heels, the diagram would show that the modifier is next to the dog, not next to her.

QUIZ

Which noun does the modifier *"they call Prince"* modify: the horse, or the sister?

> He bought a horse for his sister they call Prince.

While his sister *might* be called Prince, it's more likely to be the horse's name. He bought his sister a horse they call Prince.

12. Dangling Modifiers

Unlike a misplaced modifier, which directs attention to the wrong part of the sentence, a dangling modifier has nothing to modify. They are complete sentences, but they make no sense.

INCORRECT

- *Driving down the road,* a deer watched him carefully.
- *Youthful misdemeanors* can come back to haunt you while job hunting.

CORRECT

Modifiers offer an opportunity to go into greater detail about a subject, but the subject must be explicitly present in the sentence. Sometimes the solution is to add the missing subject, as in the first example: "As *he* drove down the road, a deer watched him carefully." Now it's clear that the deer wasn't driving down the road. In the second example, youthful misdemeanors aren't job hunting; *you* are.

MORE TO KNOW

A modifier, as an actor within a sentence, makes a small change to that sentence. It is usually descriptive, as in "dressed like a penguin," and is intended to deepen or clarify a sentence so that the reader recognizes subtlety of detail. "Dressed like a penguin, John reluctantly removed his cowboy hat and took his wife's hand as they joined the party." We can surmise that he was probably wearing a tuxedo; the modifier shines a light on his feelings.

QUIZ

What does the following sentence need for clarity?

> Coming up the stairs, the fireworks went off in all directions.

We need to know *who* is coming up the stairs; we know it isn't the fireworks.

13. Possessive Pronouns with Gerunds

This one can be tricky to get right, because the incorrect version can *sound* right to our ears. "I appreciate *you* filling in for me, Rebekah." The problem is that it's wrong. The trick is to identify the action.

INCORRECT

- Because of *me going* to the store today, I will have food for dinner.
- They always teased John about *him reading*.

CORRECT

Identify the action: I went to the store, so the going-to-the-store action was *mine,* all mine. It was *my going* to the store that enabled me to make dinner. The easy fix is "Because *I* went to the store today, *I* will have food for dinner." John was teased about *his* action; it was *his reading* that caused them to tease him, so he was teased "about *his* reading."

MEMORY TIP

A gerund is an –ing verb used as a noun (bellyaching, pontificating, roaring, etc.). They are often paired with possessive pronouns: *your* filling in, *her* roaring, *his* bellyaching. Once you understand who the action belongs to, you will remember; it will be *your* (possessive pronoun) *remembering* (gerund) that guides you to safe and correct usage.

QUIZ

Which pronouns should you use in the following sentence: *we, us,* or *our*?

> _____ dancing with wild abandon is what got _____ into trouble in the first place.

It was *our* dancing with abandon that got *us* into trouble.

14. Dual Possession

Two kinds of dual possession—with two names, and with a name and a pronoun—are stumbling blocks for even the smartest writers. Is it *Elaine's and I's* coffee pot? *Jill's and Jack's* pail of water? The rules are specific; you just need to follow them.

INCORRECT

- Our dog pounced on *Avery's and Morgan's* cat with significant consequences.
- They came to look at *Peter's and she's* car but bought another one instead.
- *Karen's and mine's* stealthy correspondence lasted many years.

CORRECT

When two people own something together—call them Avery and Morgan—then what they own is Avery and *Morgan's* property, with the apostrophe at the end of the second name of the unit of Avery and Morgan. If it's Avery's and *his* property (using a pronoun), the apostrophe is placed at the end of the first name of the unit of Avery and him; the possessive is already there in the pronoun *his*.

MEMORY TIP

Does the sentence have two names? The apostrophe goes on the second name: Jan and *Robert's* pizza. Does the sentence have a name plus a pronoun? An apostrophe belongs on the name only: *Jan's* and my pizza. Never use an apostrophe with a possessive pronoun ("my's").

QUIZ

Where would you place the apostrophes in the following sentence?

> We ate Eric_ and Michelle_ pizza before we even made it to Lori_ and his house.

The pair, "Eric and Michelle," is a unit: Eric and *Michelle's* pizza. "*Lori's* and his" house is a unit as well.

15. Double Genitive

You know what a double genitive is, even if you don't realize it. "He's *a friend of Maud's*" is an example of a double genitive. Are you a "friend of Paul," or a "friend of Paul's"? Are you a "cousin of Jamal," or a "cousin of Jamal's"?

INCORRECT

- I remember that guy; he is an acquaintance *of my uncle*.
- Hey, that mug is one *of my roommate*.
- He is a colleague *of Ruth*.

CORRECT

He is an acquaintance of *my uncle's,* not of mine. My roommate has many mugs, and that mug is his—*my roommate's.* There is some subtlety here: The apostrophe places the focus on the person. "A colleague of Ruth's" indicates that *Ruth* is the one who considers him the colleague. He is a colleague of *hers;* he is a colleague of *Ruth's.*

MORE TO KNOW

This grammatical construction is oddly controversial, but it needn't be. A double genitive indicates possession by the preposition *of* followed by the possessive form of a noun, pronoun, or name. As soon as you use *of,* as in *many of,* the *of* indicates possession: *of mine, one of his, many of the school's.* Adding the apostrophe plus the letter *s* indicates that second level of possession. It is an idiomatic construction, and it is correct. Substitute a possessive pronoun (mine, yours, his, hers, its, ours, yours, and theirs) for the name and the apostrophe plus the letter *s,* and you'll still be right.

16. Subjunctive Mood I: If I Were ...

Did you know that verbs have moods? The subjunctive mood allows you to be wishful, or to talk about something that isn't true. In *Fiddler on the Roof*, Tevye was not a rich man, but he sang about how he would spend his money *if he were* actually rich.

INCORRECT

- *If he was* going to steal that TV from you, he did a lousy job of it.
- *If our professor was* to assign grammar homework, we would all protest.

CORRECT

A sentence of this type can be wide open in time, and it can address unreal possibilities. Regardless of who is speculating, use *were*: "If he *were* going to steal that TV," or "If your professor *were* to assign homework."

MORE TO KNOW

When you use this construction—*if* ___ *were*—you open up the likelihood that something (good or bad) would have happened, might be happening, or will be happening. *If* he *were* here yesterday, he would have seen that error coming.

If you *were* here right now, you could stop that error. *If* you *were* here tomorrow, you might stop that error. *If* you *weren't* here, too bad.

17. Subjunctive Mood II: I Demand That ...

The subjunctive mood expresses a particular condition: "I hope *that* you . . . ," "I suggest *that* she . . . ," and "it's important *that* I . . ." In each case, *that* sets up an expectation for the remainder of the sentence. The challenge comes in the verb that follows that opening. Is it essential that he *write* well, or *writes* well?

INCORRECT

- She insists *that he leaves* now because he corrected her grammar.
- Management recommends *that the committee approves* the project.
- He used to command *that his underlings are* at attention at all times.

CORRECT

The tendency in this error is to conjugate the verb: "that he *leaves*," "that the committee *approves*," etc. However, the verb after *that* should always be unconjugated: leave, approve, be. She insists that he *leave* now. Management recommends that the committee *approve* the project. He commanded that his underlings *be* at attention. It's simple; I hope that you *learn.*

MEMORY TIP

A lovely consistency of this aspect of the subjunctive mood is that when it expresses commands, suggestions, and wishes, the verb that follows (eat, stir, watch, etc.) is always in present tense, regardless of the tense of the rest of the sentence. She *insisted* that you leave (past tense), she *insists* that you leave (present tense), and she *will insist* that you leave (future tense) all use "leave."

18. May and Might

Oh, the possibilities! If you use these two words interchangeably when you speak, you are not alone. *May* and *might* deal with things that are, were, or will be possible; there are subtle differences between the two that are worth knowing.

INCORRECT

- We *might* sit down to eat dinner.
- She *may* have run for president.
- The coffee *might* cool down during your meeting.

CORRECT

May is used for things that really could happen, as in "I *may* be correct." *Might* is for things that are hypothetical, as in "I *might* have driven a little too enthusiastically." It's likely that you will sit down to eat dinner, so use *may*. Few of us know people who have run for president, so use *might*. And that coffee will definitely cool down, so use *may*. If it's probable, use *may*. If it's unlikely or only vaguely possible, use *might*.

MORE TO KNOW

Consider the famous children's poem: "Star light, star bright, first star I see tonight; I wish I may, I wish I might, have the wish I wish tonight." It trained us to use *may* and *might* the same way. But if you take it (and your wish) seriously and practice daily, you *may* get your wish to perform at Carnegie Hall. If you never practice except in the shower, you *might*.

QUIZ

Should you use *may* or *might* in the following sentence?

> I just _____ have climbed Mt. Kilimanjaro in my pajamas; you weren't there so you don't know.

Mt. Kilimanjaro is cold on top, so you would have to wear more than pajamas! You just *might* have climbed Mt. Kilimanjaro.

19. Get, Got, and Gotten

This word and its variants are incredibly common and useful, and rather easily misused. It means to receive, to become, to be allowed or to have the opportunity, and to arrive. It also means possession, understanding, and obligation when paired with "have"! That is one busy word! (Have you) got it?

INCORRECT

- *I got* a twenty that says you mess up its and it's.
- He's *gotta* plan.
- When did you *got* here?

CORRECT

Get—present tense—seems fairly straightforward: I *get* paid, I *get* restless, and I *get* there on time. Adding "have" to its past participle—*got*—gives us the urgency of "I must": "I *have got* to buy books," or "I *have got* to start working." Adding "have" to *gotten*, however, serves as the standard past participle in American English: "I *have gotten* [received] a gift," "I *have gotten* [become] sick," "I *have gotten* [had the opportunity] to visit Yosemite," and "I *have gotten* [arrived] to work on time." The complication is when to use which one. If you speak American English, use *have gotten* as the past participle.

MORE TO KNOW

Gotten is a legitimate word; used with "have" (often in a contraction, as in "*I've gotten* this project off the ground"), it makes good sense to Americans and Canadians. Although it is English in origin, speakers of British English abhor its use; it fell out of favor several hundred years ago. To the English ear, it sounds like an encroaching Americanism, but it is not.

QUIZ

Should you use *got* or *gotten* in the following sentence?

> I have ______ to visit Angkor Wat and Borobudur before I die!

This sentence uses the *have got* construction to indicate obligation. I *must*! If the sentence read "I have gotten to visit [A and B] several times," it would also be correct. I *was allowed*.

20. Indefinite Pronouns: Each

Each reader of this book *is* entitled to learn about grammar, right? Or wait, should that be each of us *are* entitled to learn about grammar? Is this about me, or all of us?

INCORRECT

- Each of the three students *were* entitled to one grammatical error on the quiz.
- While I'm watching, each one of the kittens *are* falling asleep.
- Each of their grammatical errors *feel* like a knife through my heart.

CORRECT

This is actually a simple rule to learn! No matter how many numbers come after *each*, the verb must be singular: Each one of the students was entitled to an error. Ignore the number and simply connect *each* to the singular form of the verb. *Each* student *is* entitled, *each* kitten *is* falling asleep, and *each* error *feels* like a knife. Ouch! The word *each* indicates just one of two or more; that's why it is singular.

MORE TO KNOW

The word *each* is an indefinite pronoun, along with *all, any, some, none,* and many others. Some are singular (*each*), some are plural (*several*), and some can be both, as in *there is none left* and *there are none left*. Perhaps the confusion in singular/

plural words such as *none, all,* and *most* has resulted in *each* appearing equally confusing, but it isn't. *Each* uses a singular construction.

21. Helping Verbs: To Have

The simple past—*fell, broke, forgot, regretted,* etc.—is simple: The lamp *fell* and *broke*. I *forgot* the milk. Errors can creep in, however, when the helping verb *to have* is needed.

INCORRECT

- Apparently he *had ate* my dinner when he broke in.
- *I seen* him when he crept out from the kitchen.
- Zahra *agreed* to wait at the shop before she realized that her purse was at home.

CORRECT

The perfect form indicates that an action has been completed. "He *had eaten* my dinner" means that dinner is now gone. Because this construction adds an extra step in understanding, some speakers leave it out altogether, resulting in "I seen him." Others add the correct version of *have,* but neglect to shift the verb, resulting in "He had ate." When two parts of a sentence occur at different times, it can be tempting to put both parts of the sentence in the past tense, but "Zahra *had agreed*" before she realized that she didn't have her purse.

MORE TO KNOW

Adding a variant of *have* to a word in past tense turns it into a "perfect" construction. I *have fallen* (present perfect), I *had fallen* (past perfect), and I *will have fallen* (future perfect) are all variants. Some verbs change when the sentence shifts into perfect tense: *fall, have fallen; ate, have eaten; saw, have seen,* etc., but most stay the same (*regretted, have regretted*).

22. Helping Verbs: To Be

Be stands alone as a verb, and its presence changes other verbs from (for example) "I *read*" to "I *am reading*." You *are reading* this entry, since you've *been wanting* to know more about grammar, and you still need help! We all do. Even verbs can need help; that's why *to be*—the most common verb in English—is one of the helping verbs.

INCORRECT

- *They winning* at cards all evening.
- I *be sitting* next to the fire, just like a pirate. ARRR!
- You *are drink* cider again; I hope it's good.

CORRECT

Native speakers of English usually combine a subject (a noun such as a person, place, or thing), a verb (some variant of *to be*), and a present participle (going, doing, dancing, etc.) to create sentences such as "They *are drinking* cider." In some parts of the United States, people leave out the "to be" part, so rather than "They *are winning*," they would say "They *winning*." The correct form needs that helping verb!

MORE TO KNOW

Irregular verbs are old. *To be* has to be one of the oldest, as it deals with our very existence; it definitely predates Shakespeare's *Hamlet* ("to be or not to be?") from about 1600. When we use *to be* with an –ing or present participle form of another verb, as in "I *am dancing* like a disco queen," we are indicating continuous action; it's called the progressive tense.

23. Helping Verbs: To Do

We use *do*, *does*, *did*, *don't*, and *didn't* constantly; because of that, we run the risk of messing up this very irregular auxiliary verb. Have you ever heard a child say that she "dood" something, as if it were a past tense version of *do*? You wouldn't be alone in smiling at her mistake!

INCORRECT

- *Does* you want some of this carrot cake?
- He *do* think he *don't* need any help with grammar.

CORRECT

The past tense of *do* is always *did*, and the past tense of *don't* is always *didn't*. Simple! With *do* and *does*, we confuse them because of the irregularity of "I *do*" and "he does." Using "he/she *don't*" is the most common mistake of all; it should always be "he/she *doesn't*." I think he *doesn't* need any help with grammar.

MORE TO KNOW

The word *do* has so many uses! We use it to ask questions ("*Do* you like music?"), to substitute for repetitive phrases ("She plays music and so *do* I"), to emphasize something ("I *did* do the dishes!"), and to express the negative and positive ("We *don't* listen to music" and "Yes, you *do*"). Its frequent use means you'll have lots of opportunities to get this right.

24. Reflexive Pronouns: Myself

It's common to hear people use *myself* as a substitute for *me*. You might also have heard "win *theyself* a prize," or "fix *youself* some dinner." It seems like a reasonable mistake when one uses a subject pronoun (they or you), but these need *reflexive* pronouns such as *themselves* or *yourself*.

INCORRECT

- The IRS sent the refund check to my wife and *myself*.
- Be sure to notify Morgan and *myself* that you finished the paint job.
- Did you tell them that my paintings were better than those done by *theyself*?

CORRECT

A reflexive pronoun is useful in referring to the one who did the action: *myself*, *yourself/-selves*, *himself*, *herself*, *oneself*, *itself*, *ourselves*, and *themself/-selves*. For example, "I hurt *myself*" includes the subject, the verb, and the (reflexive) object. It must acquire meaning from an earlier part of the sentence. "*You* cooked it *yourself*." Sentences such as "Please give it to *myself*" are incorrect because *myself* doesn't refer to anyone. The IRS sent that check to me. I didn't do it! Neither Morgan nor I finished the paint job—you did!

MORE TO KNOW

If you use the phrase, "I've got to hand it to *myself*," that is exactly right; you did the action right back to yourself. "I'm going to decorate the room *myself*, and laugh *myself* into delirium" are completely appropriate. After all, Annie Lennox and Aretha Franklin sang in 1985 that "Sisters are doin' it for *themselves*"; *they* (pronoun) and *themselves* (reflexive pronoun).

25. Double Negatives

We can blame the Rolling Stones for teaching us that we "*can't* get *no* satisfaction," and Bob Dylan for writing the very catchy "You Ain't Going Nowhere." Those double negatives, and their variants, are ubiquitous in popular usage. Their use sometimes forces you to stop and puzzle out the positive meaning, which is never fun.

INCORRECT

- "She *didn't* want me to *not* do it."
- *Don't* give me *no* nonsense.

CORRECT

A double negative can be a simple intensifier, as in "We *didn't* do *nothing* on Saturday," or as a substitute for *any* or *anything*. We emphasize the word *nothing* to make it stronger. If you were to tell someone, "I *don't not* want you to ask me on a date," the sentence is just plain passive-aggressive (and unlikely to win you a date). Look at how difficult it is to know what that first example is communicating! The proper form is much easier to understand: "She wanted me to do it."

MORE TO KNOW

There are situations and needs that make a double negative useful. Because we often imagine that two wrongs do make a right, using two negatives can sometimes result in a positive, and the spoken emphasis makes that clear: I didn't *not* want that muffin. Sometimes the double negative serves a purpose in dramatically emphasizing a point. In *The Wizard of Oz*, Dorothy and friends arrive at the Emerald City, where they are memorably greeted with a shouted "*Not nobody*! *Not no how*!" and a slamming window.

QUIZ

Does this double negative work well, or is it an error?

> That attitude *won't* get you *nowhere*.

What? Should this be "That attitude *won't* get you *anywhere*?" Or is it an awkward and confusing way of saying that it *will* get you *somewhere*? Assume the former.

{ CHAPTER TWO }

Punctuation Saves Lives

It's amazing how one little mark can change the entire meaning of a sentence. And while we hope you'll never be in a situation in which a punctuation error will endanger your life, it may make you feel as if you've died from embarrassment.

26. Comma Usage

Sprinkling commas through one's writing as if they were candy is not a good practice. Similarly, withholding said "candy" leaves one's readers galloping too fast through the field of prose without a chance to breathe. Commas add rhythm and beauty, not to mention clarity, to one's written ideas.

INCORRECT

- The book, was lying right there; it needed to be finished.
- My friends Roderick and Anna were getting married.
- At first we wanted to eat but, we went home instead.

CORRECT

Many writers place commas wherever you might pause naturally when speaking. That's often fine, but there are specific rules to follow, and they're worth learning. Use a comma to separate independent clauses when they're joined by a conjunction (and, but, for, or, nor, so, yet). "At first we wanted to eat, but we went home instead." Use a pair of commas mid-sentence to set off clauses, phrases, and words that aren't essential. "My friends, Roderick and Anna, were getting married." Use commas to separate items in a series. "Buy apples, oranges, and bananas." Use a comma after an introductory clause, phrase, or word that comes before the main clause. "If I have time, I would really like to learn to play the banjo." Commas should never appear between a verb and its subject, as in "The book, was lying right there."

FUN FACT

Mention the Oxford comma at your peril! People have strong feelings about it, and this is often a result of their training. Journalists are taught never to use it. The Oxford comma, otherwise known as the serial comma, is the final comma in a series that comes before the word *and* or *or*. "Buy apples, oranges, and bananas" uses the Oxford comma. You'll never be wrong if you use it, and you'll avoid troubling sentences such as "I invited my parents, Joseph Stalin and Mayor Susan Smith."

QUIZ

Where would you place commas in this sentence?

> My_ friend_ Billy_ who_ hates_ grammar_ quizzes _ failed_ the_ grammar_ quiz.

My friend Billy, who hates grammar quizzes, failed the grammar quiz.

27. Comma Splice

A comma splice occurs when you divide two complete clauses with a comma. Although we may use this phrasing when we speak, it is always a mistake when you write.

INCORRECT

- Hand me the salt and pepper, the eggs are bland.
- You sat on my pastry, now I can't eat it.
- The birds come to the feeder every day, I have to refill it constantly.

CORRECT

When two clauses are related, they should be joined by a comma and a conjunction, or divided by either a semicolon or a period (if they belong in two separate sentences). If you examine the incorrect examples, you will notice that—in addition to the solution of using either a semicolon or a period—you might alternatively try using a conjunction such as *because, so*, or *and*. "You sat on my pastry, *so* now I can't eat it" works. "You sat on my pastry; now I can't eat it" also works.

MORE TO KNOW

Although a semicolon is a handy replacement in a comma splice for related clauses, one should never separate unrelated clauses with a semicolon. "The birds come to the feeder every day; tomorrow I leave for Zimbabwe" may have a nice ring to it, but the clauses have nothing to do with each other.

28. Apostrophes for Pluralization

We add *s* to nouns to make them plural: She runs with her *dogs* every morning. Adding an apostrophe before an *s* (her *dog's*) to make a noun plural is not just a bad idea; it's incorrect! Attention, sign makers everywhere!

INCORRECT

- Reading *let's* us understand other people.
- He kept seven *cat's* in his home.
- All the *neighbor's* sat around in folding *chair's*, watching the *firework's*.

CORRECT

To write about more than one item, the primary rule is to add only *-s*. For words ending in *s, x, z, ch, ss,* or *sh,* you'll need to add *-es*. Neither needs an apostrophe. This rule includes numbers (we lived there in the *'90s*), multiple uppercase letters (one can never have too many *CDs*), and names (three *Susans*). A word that is also a contraction, such as *let's* (let us) requires just a moment's thought.

MORE TO KNOW

The rule for apostrophe usage with pluralization is simple: no apostrophes! The only exception is made for clarity when you write about lowercase single letters: Mind your *p's* and *q's*; there are four *a's* in Athabaskan; and you'll need two *m's* in dilemma. The *Oakland A's* would also appreciate that apostrophe.

29. Hyphens

Hyphens have so many uses! They're often used incorrectly, either appearing where they shouldn't, or not being used when they should be. Along with comma usage, proper hyphenation is a common concern.

INCORRECT

- His boss is totally *self aggrandizing.*
- She has a *seven year old* son.
- I always use a *quarter cup* of semisweet chocolate chips in my cookies.

CORRECT

With a hyphen you may join adjectives before a noun (*weak-armed* pitcher), with compound numbers (*seven-year-old*), with fractions (*a quarter-cup*), with a prefix connected to a proper noun (*un-American*), or to enhance clarity (*de-ice*).

Lastly, use them with *half, all,* and *self* prefixes (*half-baked, all-in,* and *self-aggrandizing*). In each case, the hyphen connects two or more related words. The most important rule is that we use them to avoid confusion.

MORE TO KNOW

Don't use a hyphen if you are using just one adjective; for example, she is an African American. With two adjectives, the hyphen is required: African-American woman. Adverbs ending in –ly do not take a hyphen (as in "quickly melting chocolate"). Language changes over time, and the hyphen has not been immune; for example, we used to eat *ice-cream* and tried to avoid being stung by *bumble-bees* in the summer. Those hyphens, and many others, have disappeared and the words were either separated (*ice cream*) or brought together (*bumblebee*). The internet age influences hyphen usage too; for example, words such as *hyperlink* and *toolbar* are unhyphenated because hyphens mess with coding issues.

30. Capitalization

Noting which words should and should not be capitalized could be a full-time job. The all-or-nothing ones are simple: Always capitalize the days of the week, months, proper names, places, languages, and religions. Never capitalize the seasons. If only that were all you needed to know!

INCORRECT

- Are you heading West in the Spring?
- I saw chancellor Jones speaking with the Senator.
- My friend is a buddhist and he speaks japanese.

CORRECT

Professional titles and directions seem tricky, but the rules are actually quite simple. Capitalize titles before names, as in *Uncle* John or *President* Adrienne Smith. Do not capitalize a professional title when it appears alone (the *mayor*), or after a name, as in Ellen Jones, *company president*. For directions, your quick key is this: When you use *the* for a direction, capitalize that direction. Drive *northwest* to Seattle; you'll be in *the West*.

FUN FACT

Religions (Hinduism, Buddhism, etc.) and religious figures (Mohammed, Jesus, Buddha) are capitalized, but *atheist* and *pagan* are not.

31. Quotation Marks

In this age of "air quotes" around "words," it can be hard to "know when" to use them properly. Don't let this happen to you.

INCORRECT

- My dog barked, "Hey, as if he were trying to tell us something."
- Joe asked, Why not "buy some apples for dessert"?
- To "bee or not to bee," mused the queen of the hive.

CORRECT

Quotation marks belong in pairs around very specific sets of words: direct speech ("Why not buy some apples for dessert?"), phrases, or (quite logically) quotations ("to bee or not to bee"). We often forget to close the quotation marks, and simply keep writing as if the quoted segment continues. An entire quoted phrase, including its original punctuation, needs to be within a pair of quotation marks. In American English, additional punctuation usually goes inside the quotation marks.

MORE TO KNOW

Americans and the British use punctuation differently with quotation marks. In American English, we write "policeman." In British English, they write "bobby". Note that the period lies inside the quotation marks for one and outside for the other. When punctuation is excluded from a quoted phrase, it remains outside: Did she finish her letter by writing, "I love you, Ned"? (The letter didn't say "I love you, Ned?".) For quotation marks within a quoted phrase, use single marks: The author told me, "My editor said, 'We need an example here' for this part of the book."

32. Em Dash and En Dash

Sometimes a dash isn't just a dash. Do you know when to use a hyphen and when to use either an em or en dash? Did you know there were em and en dashes? It can be easy to confuse them, but they have unique uses.

INCORRECT

- Napoleon (1769-1821) escaped from exile, for better or worse.
- The Seahawks-Seattle's football team-won the Super Bowl at last.
- They were 15—16 years old.

CORRECT

Em dashes are the widest dash, and are so handy. They can replace parentheses—where an aside might appear—and that's not all! They can also replace commas—as long as you have a pair—in many sentences. They can even replace a colon—like this. The slightly shorter en dash serves to join a pair of numbers (1769–1821 or 15–16) or to connect two ideas (such as the Canadian–American linguistic divide). Hyphens are often mistakenly used in place of en dashes, but they have their own uses, as you already learned.

MORE TO KNOW

En dashes are the width of the letter n (–), and em dashes are the width of the letter m (—). To make them on your computer, learn these simple keystroke combinations: For Macs, press option + hyphen to make an en dash, and shift + option + hyphen (or use two hyphens) for em dash. On a PC, use ALT + 0150 (en dash) or ALT + 0151 (em dash).

QUIZ

Should the following sentence have an en dash or an em dash, or both?

> His little brother _____ who should have known better _____ stole the cookie dough.

You would need a pair of em dashes to set the internal phrase apart.

33. Ellipses

For all the fun of social media and the ease of texting, one unhappy consequence has been the overuse . . . of . . . lots of . . . periods. Put yourself on solid ground with this form of punctuation.

INCORRECT

- I told him that I wasn't going to ever......talk to him again.
- In the middle of her long speech, she said, "and that's what I needed."
- He asked for just one thing:. . . . . .

CORRECT

Whereas em dashes convey certainty—which we all would like to have when we wish to be taken seriously—ellipses can indicate some kind of . . . hesitancy. (Three dots please, not two or eight. Three.) Ellipses [plural] need a space on each side, but also (usually) between the three dots. They are also used to indicate that a quotation is just part of a longer passage: " . . . and that's what I needed."

FUN FACT

The use of the terms "three dots" and (spoken) "dot dot dot" is so common that Herb Caen, late beloved columnist for the *San Francisco Chronicle*, called his style of using ellipses between short paragraphs "Three Dot Journalism." The etymology of *ellipsis* is rooted in Greek; it means "omission."

34. Missing Accent Marks

Oh, the tragedy of writing about the delicious pate they served at last night's party. Astute readers will imagine a head on a platter, all for want of the proper accent mark.

INCORRECT

- I gave the manager my re'sume'.
- Wow! Those jalapenos really wake up the salsa!
- Garcon! Garcon!

CORRECT

Accent marks, also known as diacritical marks, indicate the specific pronunciation of a letter. In garcon, for example, the *c* would be pronounced like *k*: Garkon! No wonder he doesn't respond! Add a cedilla to that *c* and the sound changes: garçon. The server will respond to you now. You'd need a tilde over the *n* to spell and pronounce jalapeños correctly; and no matter how we might wish it to be true, apostrophes do not replace the two French accents. If you are typing in a country whose language uses these accent marks, you'll find them on the keyboard.

MORE TO KNOW

Even if you're not in a country where accent marks are common, you can still add them quite easily. If you're on an Apple (Mac) laptop, or a cellphone (regardless of whether it is an iPhone or an Android), press and hold the key for which you need the accent. On a PC, unique four-digit codes, used after you press the ALT key, create various accents. Alternatively, you can use the "Insert" toolbar, and then select "Symbol." Just don't use an apostrophe.

35. Semicolons

The much-maligned semicolon is your friend. Alas, some people use them as commas or colons, with incomplete clauses, or as part of winky-face emojis. Their true purpose, however, is to lend clarity and elegance only to those sentences in which they are needed.

INCORRECT

- I like animals; lions, tigers, and bears.
- As for the Mariners baseball team; they lost again.
- I like coffee, I would like to make some right now.

CORRECT

A semicolon separates two related but independent clauses: "I like coffee; I would like to make some right now." In a list preceded by a colon, a semicolon separates items that include commas: "I like hot drinks: coffee, because it helps me focus; and tea, because it reminds me of living in Ireland."

MORE TO KNOW

When you have a coordinating conjunction between two clauses, you don't need a semicolon. "He likes the red car, *but* she likes the gray car." However, this sentence needs a semicolon: "He likes the red car; she likes the gray car." And unlike with some colons, never capitalize the word following a semicolon.

QUIZ

Should you use a semicolon in the following sentence?

> I should have stopped by the store for coffee __ I just didn't bother.

The first clause is complete; a semicolon is necessary

36. Possessives with Names Ending in S

The Irish poet William Butler Yeats would roll over in his grave if he saw how often people wrote such egregious errors as "W.B. Yeat's poetry." Your mastery of possessives isn't complete until you understand what to do when names end in *s*.

INCORRECT

- I was startled by the attack on Yeat's poetry.
- Jameses' mom told him to sit down.

CORRECT

We are fortunate that spoken words came before written words, so we all have learned to say *Yeats's poetry* and *James's mom* before we learned to write them. Trust the way you speak! When a possessive name ends with *s* or *z*, add an apostrophe and an *s*. Say this to yourself: "I happen to love Yeats's poetry." You automatically said it correctly.

MORE TO KNOW

When the final *s* in a word is unpronounced, as in Descartes, you simply add an apostrophe without the additional *s*. "Alas, they never understood *Descartes'* philosophies." The same is true when a name ending in *s* is ancient (Socrates, Moses): Just add the apostrophe for the possessive. "I learned so much from *Socrates'* teachings."

37. Ending a Declarative Sentence with a Question Mark

People often write declarative statements such as "I wonder who wrote *The Book of Love*?" The temptation to add a question mark is great, even though the sentence is not actually a question. If you wonder who wrote *The Book of Love*, just ask the question directly.

INCORRECT

- I asked myself if this was true?
- He wondered when the train would arrive?
- Perhaps she questions her very existence?

CORRECT

The solution for this mistake is to understand the difference between a question and a declarative sentence. Declarative sentences make a statement: "I wonder who wrote *The Book of Love*." When you write a declarative sentence, regardless of the words in that sentence, you are not asking a question. Declare: "He wondered when the train would arrive." Ask: "When will the train arrive?" Declare: "She asked her teacher if she might leave." Ask: "She asked her teacher: May I leave?"

MORE TO KNOW

There are four types of sentences: declarative (making a statement), interrogative (asking questions), imperative (issuing orders), and exclamative (self-explanatory!). You wonder. He asks. They question. I do declare!

38. Colons

Do you confuse the usage of colons and semicolons? They both separate parts of a sentence, but they fill quite different needs. They also come with their own punctuation rules: Pay attention!

INCORRECT

- He gave me two things, a red wagon and a flag.
- I need: sugar, flour, and baking powder.
- In the words of Humphrey Bogart: "here's looking at you, kid."

CORRECT

A colon introduces whatever item or list of items comes next: a barrel of monkeys, a flotilla of geese, or a consternation of grammarians. It is not necessary after a verb in a sentence that needs only commas. ("I need sugar, flour, and baking powder.") Capitalize only complete clauses after colons. The examples above include three errors: a comma before a list, an unnecessary colon, and an uncapitalized complete clause after a colon.

MORE TO KNOW

When used improperly, colons can lend a different meaning than intended. "Don't let worries kill you: Let me help." As long as you use a colon before a list, before a long quotation, or before part of a sentence that explains what was just stated, you'll be fine.

QUIZ

Should you use a colon, a semicolon, or a comma in the following sentence?

> He had three options__to run, to swim, or to fly.

When you make a statement with a list, your best bet is to use a colon in front of it.

---

39. The Vocative Comma

The comma strikes again! In this case, the question is where you place the comma(s?) when you're addressing a specific person. Hail Caesar?

INCORRECT

- Greetings everybody!
- I didn't eat Jody.
- My friend you're the best person for the job.

CORRECT

The vocative comma enables you to direct attention to someone specific. By saying, "Greetings, everybody," you separate the statement of "greetings" from those addressed. It can appear anywhere in a sentence. ("I didn't eat, Jody.") How useful the vocative comma was in that sentence! Without it, I'm left wondering why you're telling me you didn't eat our friend, and suddenly I'm afraid.

FUN FACT

The word *vocative* is of Late Middle English origin by way of Old French, and before that, Latin: *vocare,* meaning "to call." The name of this comma makes perfect sense.

QUIZ

Where would you place a comma in this sentence?

> I expect you to correct your writing mistakes dear student.

Beware of any person in a position of authority who refers to you this way, dear student.

40. Pride Capitals

You might have a friend (or maybe your grandmother) who likes capital letters a little too much, even if they have no idea what a pride capital is. Now you can be specific when you teach them the error of their ways.

INCORRECT

- I gave my Oldest brother a copy of a really Great book.
- We must Fight for the right to Read!
- That book made me feel Happiness and Pride and All Good Things.

CORRECT

Pride capitals have nothing to do with the normal rules of capitalization; they exist simply as a way to emphasize particular words. In the examples, the only words that are appropriately capitalized begin each sentence. Rather than writing "I Hated that movie; it made me cry All Night," try italicizing instead: "I *hated* that movie; it made me cry *all night*." For those using capitalization arbitrarily, italics won't help. Instead, consider sticking to the rules.

MORE TO KNOW

Over-capitalization seems to run rampant when one has little to say that is genuinely important or interesting. Pride capitals are a way to emphasize without being particularly creative. For example: "I went to a Museum" uses only "went." Strong verbs are fun! Replace "went" with "meticulously explored," "rampaged through," or "danced around inside," and you won't need pride capitals to make your point. This is your chance to be creative.

41. Scare Quotes

Quotation marks around dialogue and quotations are pretty straightforward. It's increasingly common, though, to see marks around individual words or phrases. These quotations muddy the waters of sentences and confuse the minds of readers, and can be downright disturbing.

INCORRECT

- Please come and "try" our "fresh" sandwiches!
- I'd like to see him "channel" his inner Aquaman.
- We are open "24 hours a day."

CORRECT

Scare quotes are quotation marks placed around a word or phrase to signal its use in a nonstandard way or to convey irony, skepticism, or disagreement. They're also known as sneer quotes, which kind of says it all. Anyone accustomed to reading normal prose would (and probably should) pause at the door of a business that uses quotation marks around any of its products, especially "food." Scare quotes also serve the purpose of sarcasm: The four-hour lecture on punctuation was "interesting."

FUN FACT

The Ancient Greeks used a version of scare quotes. And although their usage disappeared for a long time, they've had a resurgence starting in the 1990s.

42. Punctuation for Currency

Photographs of terribly mistaken signs from shops all over the country appear online, provoking great laughter and embarrassment when a manager discovers that rather than offering bananas for ten cents each, he is offering bananas for one-tenth of a cent each. What a bargain!

INCORRECT

- We are selling pens today for .90¢.
- I paid 4,000$ for my used car.
- 99¢ almost equals a single penny.

CORRECT

Our main symbols for currency are the dollar symbol ($), the cents symbol (¢), and the decimal point (.). The dollar sign appears before the amount: $15.25. The trouble begins when we deal with amounts of less than a dollar. You may write *$0.99* or *99¢*, both of which mean 99 cents. Any sum with a decimal point and a ¢, however, signifies less than a penny.

MORE TO KNOW

It helps to be aware of other currencies. Internationally, the US dollar is written as USD20/US$20. The euro (€20) is in use in most of Europe, the pound (£20) is specific to the United Kingdom, and the yen (¥20) is used in Japan. In each case, we speak the number first (twenty) followed by the currency (dollars, euros, pounds, yen, etc.).

QUIZ

Which one of these accurately represents 50 cents?

$50 $0.50 .50¢

Only the middle one represents 50 cents; the left is 50 dollars, and the right is half of a single cent.

43. Apostrophes for Holidays

We celebrate many nonreligious holidays. Some of these special days include apostrophes, but others do not, and there's a simple rule to help you remember which is which.

INCORRECT

- I got her some flowers for Mothers Day.
- Happy New Year's!
- We celebrate Veteran's Day on the first Monday in November.

CORRECT

Only Mother's Day, Father's Day, Valentine's Day, and New Year's Day need an apostrophe because they are possessive; there are holidays in honor of each parent (yours), one Valentine (yours), and one New Year. Veterans Day, also known as Armistice Day, is in honor of all military veterans; it does not belong to anyone, and does not take an apostrophe. The day of the new year is New Year's Day. To be precise, without the word *day*, "Happy New Year's" means "Happy New Year is," but colloquial use allows for Happy New Year's.

FUN FACT

The first American Mother's Day was celebrated in 1908 by Anna Jarvis, who campaigned for it to be a national holiday; it happened in 1911. She noted that it is a singular "Mother's Day" (not Mothers' Day). Father's Day wasn't official until 1966.

44. Run-On Sentences

Have you ever known a person who can just keep talking and the subjects shift and change before you ever get a word in it's time to talk about how not to be tragic with run-on sentences.

INCORRECT

- I made a pot of coffee I drank it.
- She skipped grammar class she returned home with failing grades.
- His dog is a good dog he doesn't know how to punctuate a sentence.

CORRECT

A run-on sentence uses at least two independent clauses that are not connected properly. A run-on sentence needs a little tender loving care, or at least a comma, period, or semicolon. "I made a pot of coffee, *and* I drank it." Punctuation is a grand addition to any sentence with two or more independent clauses.

MORE TO KNOW

You have lots of options with run-on sentences. You can break up a run-on sentence with a period or a semicolon. You can also add a comma and a coordinating conjunction, as in "She skipped grammar class, *and* she returned home with failing grades." A semicolon and a conjunctive adverb such as *however* would work as well: "His dog is a good dog; *however*, he doesn't know how to punctuate a sentence."

QUIZ

What kind of punctuation would you add to the following run-on sentence?

> They told me that they sold the house they had lived in it for years.

Use a semicolon or a period after the word *house*.

45. Double Spaces After a Period

Once upon a time, students who learned how to type on a typewriter—you've heard of those, right?—were trained to add two spaces after a period under penalty of death. Not getting a gold star was tragic.

INCORRECT

- *Look! This* laptop won't even let me type two spaces without marking the error.
- Using two spaces looks *odd. Wide open. Bizarre.*
- Using a single space looks *clean. It's tidy. Oops*, I did it again!

CORRECT

The good people who created modern word-processing software decided that computers would be able to slightly expand the space after a period, to save its users from that extra thumb action. This has been true for decades, now that we have moved from monospace (one character per space) to proportional space (lovely kerning that makes the words fit together nicely). Save yourself unnecessary work and join the twenty-first century: one space after all sentence-ending punctuation!

FUN FACT

Irish and Anglo-Saxon monks developed spacing between words at about the same time that they were singing plainchant in monasteries: 600 CE and beyond. It made reading much easier, and became the norm by the Renaissance. There was usually an extra space after the period to separate sentences; the use of two spaces wasn't standard until the 1970s.

{ CHAPTER THREE }

Word to the Wise

If *irregardless* "literally" makes your skin crawl, this chapter is for you. Read on to learn how to avoid tragic word mix-ups and misuses.

46. Sex vs. Gender

Is it just our cultural awkwardness at using the word *sex* that makes us stick with the word *gender* to cover all the bases? Or possibly it's just a matter of uncertainty that makes us choose one or the other.

INCORRECT

- They had a party to reveal the *gender* of the unborn baby.
- The *sex* of my sister has changed over time.
- It is pretty easy to determine the *gender* of honeybees.

CORRECT

Let's be clear: *Sex* is exclusively about biology, and *gender* is about social roles and identity. We are becoming increasingly familiar with individuals who identify as a gender that doesn't align with the sex that they were assigned at birth. An unborn baby has no gender to reveal, but its sex is either male, female, or occasionally intersex (having the physical characteristics of both). So, yes, we may wish to rethink calling it a "*gender* reveal party." And as far as we know, honeybees do not express gender identities, so we're determining their sex only.

MORE TO KNOW

Derived from the Latin word *genus* (kind, family, type, etc.), the meaning of *gender* separated from the meaning of *sex* in the twentieth century. Now generally associated with identity, the social concept of gender has real-life usages and implications. Sex, which is connected etymologically with the word *section,* is about the actual biological characteristics that divide individuals.

47. Weather vs. Climate

These two words, and their implications for our survival, appear on the news every day. We talk about the *weather* and *climate* as if they are the same thing, and this confusion explains why some people dismiss climate change when the weather is cold.

INCORRECT

- Look, it's snowing! Our *climate* is chilly today.
- The *weather* hasn't changed for over five hundred years.
- How is the *climate* where you live this winter?

CORRECT

If you make a snowball and throw it, the recipient will become acutely aware of today's *weather* and how it enabled you to fashion a (mostly) harmless weapon in seconds. Changes in the *weather* are visible out your window, and measurable on your outdoor thermometer. *Climate* changes over decades and centuries, not days. If you build a house at sea level today, you will need significant insurance because your house may fall victim to global *climate* change.

MORE TO KNOW

Climate refers primarily to a zone of the earth, and is a large-scale characterization of a condition; it used to refer primarily to the angle of the sun in regard to a large region. "How was the *climate* in Mesopotamia?" refers to general characteristics. If you wanted to know about the *weather* on a particular day in Mesopotamia, you'd have to go back in time.

48. Like vs. Such As

For such a nice word, *like* causes a lot of headaches, even aside from its overuse, *like,* in everyday speech. When you want to provide an example of a category, or offer a comparison, do you use *like,* or *such as*?

INCORRECT

- He enjoys reading poems *like* "On Turning Ten" by Billy Collins.
- A guitar is *such as* a lute.
- They refuse to focus on challenging topics *like* English grammar.

CORRECT

Do you need an equivalency (*like*), or an inclusive category (*such as*)? Lemons are *like* limes; limes are *like* grapefruits. Using *such as*, on the other hand, gives you an inclusive set of categories. I enjoy all types of citrus fruits, *such as* lemons, limes, and grapefruits. *Like* is not inclusive; when you say that you love listening to songs *like* "Singing in the Rain," you are saying that you *don't* actually listen to that song. You just listen to songs *like* it. If you say that you love listening to songs *such as* "Singing in the Rain," suddenly a whole array of catchy songs will appear in the listener's mind, never to depart.

MORE TO KNOW

Many beginning writers throw in a comma after *like* or *such as*. "He has been to places like, Newfoundland" and "I lived in countries such as, Indonesia, Germany, and Ecuador" include an unnecessary comma. They were perfect without it! Your sentence is either equivalent or inclusive, and that is all you need to determine.

QUIZ

Should the following sentence include *like* or *such as* to be correct?

> Do I like pie?!? I love pies ______ apple pie, marion-berry pie, and strawberry pie.

If you wish to include all pies, and I hope you do, choose *such as*.

---

49. Irregardless

There is something inherently rebellious about the word *regardless*. It means ignoring the rules, being feisty, and offering no regard to the way things should be done. Maybe that's why people want to change it.

INCORRECT

- *Irregardless* of what you want, your parents' minds are made up.
- I have put my foot down and will use poor grammar, *irregardless*!

CORRECT

The best thing about *regardless* is its devil-may-care attitude. It implies that one is a free spirit who cares about neither grammar nor propriety. When you push it further by turning a perfectly good word into a double negative—irregardless—you immediately cross over into risky grammatical territory. Stick with *regardless* and you'll never be wrong.

FUN FACT

Merriam-Webster's website refers to *disirregardlessers* as "a small and polite group." Count yourself among them! You always mean *regardless*, regardless of how rebellious you wish to appear.

50. Set vs. Sit

As any fan of Scrabble knows, one little letter can make all the difference. Furthering the confusion between *set* and *sit* is the fact that they're often pronounced similarly. It's time to *set* things straight—you may need to *sit* down for this!

INCORRECT

- Look at him, *setting* there.
- *Sit* that lottery ticket right here.
- She couldn't *set* down fast enough.

CORRECT

Sit is one of the first verbs that children and dogs learn. Because it's so direct and almost primal in its immediacy, let it be your first choice when your body is involved. When you *sit* down, your action is complete. *Set* is for other things: objects, teacups, and lottery tickets. When you *set* something down, you need an item—a lottery ticket, for example—to place on the table.

MORE TO KNOW

Sit is an intransitive verb, which means that it is complete as is, and it doesn't need an object. *Set* is transitive, which means it always needs to connect to an object in the sentence to be correct. Transitive verbs transfer action to an object, whether it's a teacup or a great book.

QUIZ

Should you use *sit* or *set* in the following sentence?

> After playing games on my cell phone for three hours, I finally _____ it aside.

The correct answer is *set*.

---

51. Lay vs. Lie

Chickens *lay* eggs, and philosophers *lie* in bed at night, wondering which came first. The answer to that question won't help you know which word to use, but this book will.

INCORRECT

- Those cats were just *laying* all over the furniture.
- You can *lie* that spare change right on the counter.
- She said she needed to *lay* down for a bit.

CORRECT

Much like *sit* and *set*, one is done with your body and one is done to an object. You *lie* on the bed. You *lay* the pillow on the bed. As you now know, *lay* is a transitive verb so it needs some kind of object. Present tense is so easy! Those cats are *lying* on the furniture, and she needs to *lie* down. First, though, she should *lay* that spare change on the counter.

MORE TO KNOW

This word pair becomes tricky when you need past tense: I *lay* [past tense of *lie*] on the couch all day, but first I *laid* [past tense of *lay*] the cat on a pillow. I *had laid* [past participle of *lay*] the cat there before, and when she *had lain* [past participle of *lie*] there long enough, she pounced on me.

QUIZ

Which word is correct in the following sentence: *lay* or *lie*?

> When I read a social media meme with grammatical errors, I need to _______ down.

You *lie* down; you don't *lay* down, unless you are a very unusual chicken.

52. Unique

We've all had that friend who insists that her baby is really, really unique. However, unless there's something truly exceptional about the child, your friend is probably just exhibiting an especially acute case of Proud Parent Syndrome.

INCORRECT

- We visited a *unique* beach; it had sand, seaweed, and saltwater.
- This restaurant had great food; it was quite *unique*.
- Visiting my mother is an incredibly *unique* experience.

CORRECT

There is only one Mona Lisa in the world, and one Leaning Tower of Pisa. You are unique; as dear Mister Rogers used to say, "There is no one quite like you." Something unique cannot be replicated. It is the only one of its kind. A thing or experience cannot be *very unique, quite unique,* or *incredibly unique,* because *unique* is unique. On the other hand, there is nothing unique about a beach that has sand, seaweed, and saltwater.

MEMORY TIP

The best way to think of unique is to remember its Latin etymology: *one*. There is only one; it is unique. Even identical twins are unique because their life experiences differ. With that singularity of meaning, suddenly *one* seems to hold more value. Wouldn't you value something if it were the only one in the world?

53. Will vs. Shall

Shall sounds rather old-fashioned; telling someone what you *shall* and *shall not* do may sound as if you are speaking to a staff member at your castle. It is, however, entirely correct to use *shall* in certain circumstances.

INCORRECT

- I solemnly swear that I *will* stay away from the drinks tonight.
- Oooh, this is my favorite song! *Will* we dance?
- The dog *shall* eat all his food unless you put it away.

CORRECT

Sometimes we shy away from verbs that appear only occasionally in spoken English. Because it is primarily limited to the first person, about something in the future, *shall* sounds odd, even though it's correct. It isn't uncommon to hear *shall* in a question: "*Shall* we dance?" We tend to replace it (casually) with "I am going to [do X]," or "Could we [do X]?"

While still common in England and other parts of the English-speaking world, *shall* is rapidly disappearing in the United States.

MORE TO KNOW

These two words belong to the category of modal verbs; such verbs express possibility, obligation, permission, and ability. *Shall* is related to *should* just as *will* is related to *would*: definite vs. maybe. *Shall* and *will* indicate that something will happen, whereas *should* and *would*, the semi-modals, offer the possibility. Note: You *will* receive bonus points if you stamp your foot while using *shall*.

QUIZ

Does *shall* or *will* belong in this sentence?

> Since everyone here persists in using "irregardless," I _____ take my drink elsewhere.

I *shall* take my drink elsewhere; they, however, *will* persist in using "irregardless."

54. Than vs. Then

Again, one letter can make all the difference (see Set vs. Sit, page 75), when it comes to clear communication. Just think about the potentially tragic scenario you're walking into by claiming you'd rather warm up by the fireside *then* go out barefoot in the snow.

INCORRECT

- First your friend stole my guitar, *than* he played it on live television!
- I would rather be vindicated privately *then* humiliated in public.
- They ate more lunch *then* I did.

CORRECT

Then can be used to indicate a sequence ("He stole my guitar, and *then* played it"), or it can mean therefore ("If I drink a lot of water, *then* I won't eat so much"); in addition ("The cake was good, and *then* there was the frosting"); or at that time ("Come over next week; we'll have lunch *then*"). *Than* is used for comparison ("They ate more *than* I did"), but can also express preference ("I would rather play music *than* wash the dishes").

MEMORY TIP

Link *then* with time and *than* with comparisons, and you'll never mess them up again. If you use *then* to indicate a sequence (first A, then B) and *than* to indicate a comparison (A has more X than B), you're in rock-solid territory.

55. Less vs. Fewer

If you cringe at the sight of a "10 items or less" sign in a grocery store, you are a true grammarian! If you think the sign is correct, read on.

INCORRECT

- I would never ask for *less* potato chips.
- We need more light in this room, not *fewer*.
- *Less* grammar mistakes are something to strive for.

CORRECT

Less is for uncountable quantities such as water, heat, and air. Use *fewer* for countable items such as groceries, pets, or puzzle pieces. One may drink more or *less* hot cocoa while eating more or *fewer* potato chips. We are asked to use *less* salt, not *fewer* salt, and to make *fewer* mistakes, not *less*. Notice that *more* is the common oppositional point between *less* and *fewer*, and that is where the confusion lies.

FUN FACT

This distinction between *less* and *fewer*—in common usage, at least—has minimized over time, but your average grocery store express lane is one of the places where the error stands out most prominently. Just don't mention it to the clerk, as we'd all rather spend *less* time in line.

56. Loose vs. Lose

You don't have to pull your hair out over this one. Saying the words out loud will guide you to the correct choice.

INCORRECT

- His tie was too *lose*.
- Time to *loose* that smile, buster; I'm handing back your grammar exam.
- Poor word choice can make you look like a *looser*.

CORRECT

Letting your dog *loose* in the park so that it can run with other dogs illustrates the most common use of the word: as an adjective. As a verb, the word *loose* means "to release something." When you *loose* your dog, keep an eye out so that you don't *lose* it. When you *lose* something, whatever you had is no longer there. If you can't find your dog, you might *lose* hope.

MEMORY TIP

Lose (pronounced "looze") slows you down when you say it; it is as if you've lost something. Try it: looooooze. *Loose* (pronounced "lūce") is fast! Run free! You know the difference now!

QUIZ

Which word should you use in the following sentence?

> If I were to enter a grammar contest, the other people would definitely_____.

The correct answer is *lose*.

---

57. Literally

If you genuinely believe that you're literally going to die from reading this book, put it down now! I would literally cry my eyes out if you died . . . or would I?

INCORRECT

- I was *literally* sweating bullets over that grammar test.
- When she saw me with her husband, she was *literally* shooting darts at me.
- My dad *literally* fell apart laughing when he watched *The Tonight Show*.

CORRECT

The best way to know whether or not one should use *literally* in one's writing is this: Could it really happen? When you make a statement with *literally*, you remove all doubt. This thing is actually going to happen. If she *literally* shoots darts at you when she sees you with her husband, duck! We should probably use *literally* only as frequently as we use the word *unique*.

FUN FACT

The Latin root of *literal*—to the letter—brings with it the assumption of perfect and absolute truth. To do something *literally* means to distinguish it from a metaphor.

58. Number and Amount

In the amount of time it will take you to learn this rule, you could easily create a list that includes any number of correct examples.

INCORRECT

- What *amount* of children do you have?
- The glass held a surprisingly large *number* of wine.
- I can't begin to count the *amount* of times that I tried that card trick and failed.

CORRECT

Think of this pair of words in the same way you might consider *fewer* vs. *less*: One is for countable items (*number*), and the other is for uncountable items (*amount*). By now you have read a specific *number* of entries in this book; what *amount* of knowledge have you gained?

MORE TO KNOW

The word *amount* is called a mass noun, meaning that it measures uncountables such as giddiness, water in the ocean, or the northern lights. A person or an item can also "*amount* to something" (amount = verb), meaning "become equal to." "My efforts in the kitchen *amounted* to only eleven cookies after I ate one." The original *number* of cookies was twelve, after all.

QUIZ

Should the following sentence use *amount* or *number*?

> Hey, I need to borrow some random _____ of cash.

Neither a borrower nor a lender be . . . regardless of the *amount*.

59. Could of/Should of/Would of

Almost everyone says "could've," "should've," and "would've" when they speak casually to one another. It is the lucky few among those speakers who realize what the sound at the end of the words *could, should,* and *would* stands for.

INCORRECT

- I *could of* been a contender.
- You *would of* loved me if I wrote better.
- He *should of* seen that coming.

CORRECT

The substitution of *of* in place of *have* comes directly from the way we speak. When spoken out aloud, "I *should've* attended your party" sounds like "I *should of* attended your party." You're safe if you write these as contractions, but if you spell it in two words, be sure to use *have*. You should *have* seen that coming.

MORE TO KNOW

The construction *should have* + the past participle (*gone, stayed, said,* etc.) and its siblings are all past modal verbs that describe something that did not happen in the past. They all carry a tinge of regret, don't they? Perhaps we should ask ourselves why we have three different words for something that didn't happen, for which we feel a little bit bad.

60. A Lot vs. Alot

This mistake shows up all the time. In fact, it shows up quite a lot.

INCORRECT

- My professor corrects my grammar *alot.*
- Wow, there sure are *alot* of errors in this book!
- I think about chocolate *alot,* but not so much about caramel.

CORRECT

"Alot" is not a word in the English language, yet many people persist in writing *a lot* as "alot," as if it were right and normal to do so. As a unit of measurement, *a lot* was an object that stood in for a share of something else. When you ask for *a lot* of chocolate, the assumption is that there is even more to go around. You aren't eating all the chocolate, but you are eating *a lot*—an allotment—of it.

MEMORY TIP

Alot isn't a word. It's not *a lot* to remember.

61. Weather vs. Whether vs. Wether

These are three radically different concepts that are confused with each other in a startlingly frequent manner. They sound identical, but that's about all they have in common.

INCORRECT

- He liked her, *wether* or not she liked him.
- I'm trying to decide *weather* I should go to the store now or later.
- It's a good thing they all came in from the awful *whether*.

CORRECT

It's definition time. *Weather* is a noun that refers to what is happening outside: rain, sun, wind, and other conditions. *Whether* is a conjunction that offers just one alternative: whether or not. Finally, although you may not use it frequently, a *wether* is a castrated goat or ram, just as a *steer* is a castrated bull and a *gelding* is a castrated stallion. If you live on a farm, you might look out the window to check on the *wether*, but it's more likely that you're interested in the *weather*.

FUN FACT

Because a *wether* tends to hang out with the rest of the flock—as opposed to wandering off to look for potential conquests—shepherds often attach a bell to a collar around its neck. If you listen for that bell, you can find the rest of the animals and tell which direction they're headed. A *bell-wether*, then, is a harbinger of something else.

62. Breath vs. Breathe

Some nouns need only an *e* at the end to become verbs. *Breath* is one of those, and the sound of the word will lead you to the correct spelling.

INCORRECT

- Let go! I need to *breath*!
- His *breathe* was ragged.
- You say you don't want to spread your cold, yet you *breath* all over me?!

CORRECT

We can easily hear the distinction between these two words. We always pronounce them correctly. However, we don't appear to see the distinction as we write the words. To take a *breath* (noun), you need to *breathe* (verb). If all else fails, read the sentence aloud and you'll know which spelling you need.

MORE TO KNOW

Several other word pairs—*cloth* and *clothe, sooth* and *soothe,* and *loath* and *loathe*—follow the same pattern. In each case, the noun (*breath* or *cloth*) is pronounced with a strong "th" sound, such as with the word *teeth.* The verb, however (*breathe* or *clothe* or *soothe*), is pronounced with a soft "the" sound, as in *teethe.* Do you see what I did there?

QUIZ

Should you use *breath* or *breathe* in the following sentence?

> She was so allergic to her own feline assistant that she struggled to _____.

She struggled to *breathe* when she was near her cat, so she had to take medication.

63. Comprise

Many of us long to be considered a bit more educated, erudite, and complex than we actually are. Naturally, we choose fancy-sounding words; just as naturally, we misuse them with abandon and correct others who attempt to set us straight. *Comprise* is one such word, and it is incumbent upon us to use it properly.

INCORRECT

- My apple pie *is comprised of* apples, sugar, sherry, spices, and bay leaf.
- His CD collection ran the gamut from A to B; it *was comprised of* classic rock.
- The assignment *will be comprised of* research, stalling, writing, and fretting.

CORRECT

Comprise means "to consist of." When you write or say *comprised of*, you have an extra "of" in there. The result is, tragically, "comprised of of." Instead of writing apple pie is *comprised of of* apples and other ingredients, simply write apple pie *comprises* apples and other ingredients. Presto!

MEMORY TIP

From Latin, "to include or consist of," *comprise* is complete as is. The trick to using it properly is to substitute it for the word *include(s)*. My students' essays *comprise* good ideas and grammatical errors, while my colleagues' ideas *comprise* good ideas and the research to back them up.

64. Everyday vs. Every Day

Unlike the tragic "alot," both words in this pair are real words with different uses. *Every day* brings new solutions for our *everyday* problems.

INCORRECT

- I go to the mailbox *everyday*.
- My *every day* issue is locating my keys.
- My habit is to have cream in my coffee *everyday*.

CORRECT

If you read sections of this book *every day*, your *everyday* grammar skills will improve. The first one—*every day*—is the same as "each and every day" in that the days can be counted, one by one. I take vitamins *every day*. An *everyday* occurrence is something that is normal, mundane, and common. My *everyday* issue is locating my keys. Nothing about an *everyday* experience is out of the ordinary; it is the usual thing.

MORE TO KNOW

The same logic applies for *some day, some time,* and *any time.* Note, however, that it doesn't work for *any day,* because "anyday" is not something we ever say.

QUIZ

Would you choose *everyday* or *every day* for use in the following sentence?

> I am shocked by the news when I open the newspaper
>
> _____.

Reading the paper is an *everyday* (normal) experience, but it happens *every day* (correct answer).

65. There/They're/Their

There is no excuse for messing up these three words just because they sound the same. *Their* meanings do not overlap, so just take a moment to think about which one you need. *They're* not too difficult to master!

INCORRECT

- I spent the night in *there* kitchen, dancing!
- *They're* is a huge spider next to the toilet.
- Did you hear that *their* heading to Australia?

CORRECT

When it isn't used to indicate a place ("over there"), at the beginning of a sentence, *there* is called an *existential pronoun*. They tend to weaken a sentence ("There is rain"), and they're best omitted. The apostrophe in *they're* indicates a contraction: they are. *Their* derives from Old Norse, "of them," which makes sense, since it's the possessive form of *they*. "*Their* parents are so glad they finally married." Even though they sound alike, separate them in your mind when you write them out.

MORE TO KNOW

This issue belongs within the category of Homophones from Hell. *Their* and *there*, in particular, sound identical in much of the English-speaking world; *they're* is sometimes closer to "they-r" in pronunciation. Because of the fact that we speak them much more often than we write them, making them distinct in writing is usually the least of our worries.

QUIZ

Which word should you use: *they're*, *their*, or *there*?

> _____ going to set the candy right _____ in front of _____ kids!

They're going to decide, right *there*, to regret *their* decision.

66. Etc. vs. Ext.

Just as they do with the word *espresso*, people frequently—and incorrectly!—add an *x* to *etc.* when they say it. Spelling errors occur just as frequently.

INCORRECT

- I like to add cinnamon, nutmeg, *ect.* to my coffee.
- They visited Japan, Thailand, China, *ext.*

CORRECT

The abbreviation *etc.* is from Latin, *et cetera,* which means "and the rest." When you say it correctly, you actually pronounce the *et* of *et cetera,* just as Yul Brynner did in *The King and I:* "et cetera, et cetera, et cetera!" The problem is that so many people say it incorrectly as "ex cetera," and those same people write it incorrectly as either *ext.* or *ect.* (*ext.*, of course, is an abbreviation of *extension*).

MORE TO KNOW

Moving from speaking the *t* of *et* to the *c* of *cetera* is a small challenge because *t* and *c* are close together in the mouth; people go straight to *ex cetera.* The hard *c* and *x* are in the back of the throat, so the movement from there to the front of the mouth is easier, but still wrong. Finally, a note on punctuation: The period after *etc.* serves as the final period in a sentence when it comes at the end.

67. Historic/Historical

If you graduated from college, your graduation is now *historical*. If you never expected to graduate because you spent your wayward youth wearing lampshades over your head at parties, perhaps that graduation would count as *historic* for you alone. These words are not used interchangeably.

INCORRECT

- The abolition of slavery was a *historical* event.
- His participation in the Boy Scouts was *historic*.
- The formation of the European Union was *historical*.

CORRECT

Historic is used specifically for events that have been important. The San Francisco earthquake of 1906 was *historic*; the stock market crash of 1929 was also *historic*. Anything *historical* has to do with some particular time in the past. That pile of dusty papers in one's study from 1998 are anything but *historic*; they are merely *historical*. No matter how momentous and surprising your high school graduation may have been, it doesn't count as *historic*.

FUN FACT

You may hear people use the article *an* in front of historic (or historical). This is a result of British English speakers' tendency to drop the initial *h* in words like *hour* and *honor*. In American English, you can use *a* before historic/historical event, because we pronounce the initial *h*.

QUIZ

Should you use *historic* or *historical* in the following sentence?

> If Gondwana were ever reunited, that would be a _____ event.

Considering that Gondwana existed 180 million years ago, the possibility of the tectonic plates coming back together would be both *historic* and quite dramatic!

---

68. Between vs. Among

You're trying to divide your pizza into equal parts to share with people in your office, one of whom is a grammarian. Are you sharing them *between* or *among* your colleagues? You know that grammarian will be paying attention.

INCORRECT

- I ran *between* the crowd in search of my friend.
- A sense of unease began to grow *between* the class.
- He sat *among* his dog and his cat.

CORRECT

Between is for specific people (or things, or generic items), and *among* is for vague numbers. You may use *between* for many items, as long as they are specific. For example, if you had five teenagers but just one car, you might have to choose *between* Bob, Ann, Lamont, Jane, and Willoughby to determine who could borrow it first. The car would not be shared *among* all the teens, but would pass from teen to teen. If you choose *between* three people for tickets to go hear a favorite musician, jealousy might spread *among* all your other friends.

MORE TO KNOW

The division between these two words conveys a sense of direction as well as an amount. You can move *between* the dogs on the trail or *among* the dogs on the trail; in the first instance, you have a sense of forward motion by approaching and dividing a pair. In the second instance, you wander *surrounded by* all the dogs.

69. That/Which/Who

This is one of the most common mistakes that editors see, and that writers hesitate over. Although the actual rule might seem confusing, there is an easy way to keep these straight.

INCORRECT

- This is the man *that* stole my surfboard.
- The surfboard, *who* I bought in Honolulu, was precious to me.
- It had special markings *which* named me as the owner.

CORRECT

That is for elements *that* identify a subject, as in "It had special markings *that* named me as the owner." *Which* is for nonessential clauses in sentences (and are often separated from the rest of the sentence by commas): "The surfboard, *which* I bought in Honolulu, was precious to me." *Who* is for people only: "That is the man *who* stole my surfboard."

MEMORY TIP

Clarifying information that helps the sentence make sense is the reason we use *that, which,* and *who.* If it's essential, use *that.* If it's nonessential, use *which.* If you discuss people, use *who.*

QUIZ

Select *that, which,* or *who* to complete the following sentence.

> I shoved both hands, _____ I had just washed, right into the mud to locate my ring.

The hands, *which* I had just washed, became even muddier than before I washed them.

70. Its and It's

This is one of the most common slip-ups, and happens occasionally to even the most seasoned of writers. People tend to sneak the apostrophe in for either form, perhaps because *it's* occurs more frequently in writing, so it looks weird without one. Or it could be that they learned that every possessive form has an apostrophe.

INCORRECT

- Look, Mom! *Its* a beautiful sunset tonight for spying on the neighbors.
- That horse just flattened *it's* ears; stop calling it a donkey.
- The popcorn popper just blew *it's* lid.

CORRECT

Its is possessive, now and forever. It cannot be anything other than a possessive construction. *It's* always means *it is* or *it has*. It cannot be anything other than *it* + *is* or *it* + *has*. "*It is* a beautiful sunset, and the popper just blew *its* lid." Grammarians will blow their lids if you keep messing this up.

MEMORY TIP

If you aren't sure whether you've used the right word, substitute *it is* or *it has*, and see if either of those work. If so, use the apostrophe. Otherwise, no apostrophe!

71. Whose and Who's

This tragic error is similar to the *its* and *it's* problem, and luckily for you, the solution is just as simple. Pay attention to the apostrophe and you'll know which one to choose.

INCORRECT

- *Whose* on first?
- I can't even tell *whose* there because the lights are too low.
- *Who's* crab cakes were left in the fridge over the weekend?

CORRECT

Both *whose* and *who's* have at their root the pronoun *who*. Whether you intend to say *whose* or *who's* is irrelevant when you speak because they sound the same. However, they must be distinct from one another in writing. As with *its* and *your* (two other possessive pronouns), *whose* never takes an apostrophe. By contrast, *who's* always takes an apostrophe to show that it is a contraction of *who is*.

MEMORY TIP

Would the sentence make sense with *who is*? If so, use that contraction! "He's the man *who's* responsible for throwing a neighborhood party." If not, you'll need *whose*: "He's the man *whose* dog ate all the hors d'oeuvres."

72. Your and You're

The alleged intimacy of social media tempts many of us to make cryptic comments on each other's posts, such as "LOL *your* funny." The person merrily scrolls down to the next post while the rest of us recoil in horror, stammering "my funny WHAT"?!?" Meanwhile, the next comment might be "I spotted *you're* error, dude!"

INCORRECT

- Say, did you bring *you're* Einstein action figure?
- My friend says that *your* not as funny as you look.
- Be careful; *your* about to tip over.

CORRECT

Your is a possessive pronoun, and possessive pronouns do not need an apostrophe. You should notice a pattern here, connected with *its* and *whose*. Once you lose *your* way, your dog may have lost *its* way as well. Luckily, you can't lose *your* apostrophes because you don't need them. Because *you're* always means *you are*, it has nothing to do with possession. The contraction needs an apostrophe, as they always do, and the possessive pronoun does not.

MEMORY TIP

This tip is familiar by now: Substitute *you are* and decide whether it makes sense in the context of the sentence. Correct: *You're* ("you are"?) a brilliant and grammatically correct role model for us all! Incorrect: *You're* ("you are"?) grammar posts make no sense, so stick with "*your* grammar posts."

73. i.e. and e.g.

Any time we directly import Latin words (such as *et cetera*, as we've already seen, and *ipso facto*, *per se*, or *ergo*) into our writing, we run the risk of embarrassing ourselves. Even though they're just two letters each, *i.e.* and *e.g.* seem to cause a lot of confusion.

INCORRECT

- My students need help with grammar; *e.g.*, they forget grammar rules.
- The buffet included plenty of options (*i.e.*, chicken, steak, and fish).
- The store is closed, *e.g.*, shut down for good.

CORRECT

The Latin phrase *id est*, abbreviated *i.e.*, means "that is." The Latin phrase *exempli gratia*, abbreviated *e.g.*, means "for example." When using *i.e.* and *e.g.* in a sentence, use a comma or semicolon before and a comma after, as in "David loves to travel; i.e., he has an adventurous spirit." Note that the last phrase is complete. You may also use parentheses: "Our neighborhood deer love to eat vegetation (*e.g.*, grass, leaves, twigs)."

MEMORY TIP

Your best bet in remembering the difference between these two is to think about *i.e.* as standing for "in essence," and the *e* of *e.g.* as "example."

QUIZ

Should you use *e.g.* or *i.e.* in the following sentence?

> My 87-year-old mother understands textspeak, ___, LOL, BRB, and IKR.

Because LOL, BRB, and IKR are *examples* of textspeak, use *e.g.*

74. A While and Awhile

Has it been awhile since you thought about how you use *awhile* and *a while*? Even if it seems as if you are allowed to use them interchangeably, thou shalt not!

INCORRECT

- He has wasted their time *for awhile* and he needs to stop.
- I need you to sit and practice your euphonium *a while*.
- I'll give you your allowance *in awhile* if you are patient.

CORRECT

Our internal haze about which one is correct under which circumstances has to do with the fact that they sound exactly alike when we say them out loud. *Awhile* can appear right after a verb—*wait awhile, read awhile, dance awhile*—while (ha!) the second, *a while,* needs a preposition such as *for, after,* or *in* to be complete. Let's think about this *for a while*. I'll get to your question *in a while. Stay awhile* so we can chat *for a while.*

MORE TO KNOW

The grammatical key behind *awhile* and *a while* is that *awhile* is an adverb, and *a while* is a noun phrase: a noun (*while*) + an article (*a*). Notice that if you use the colloquial "sit here for a spell," nothing could tempt you to write "for aspell." You automatically use *for*, and you separate *a* and *spell*: three separate words of "for a spell." Write *for a while* the same way.

QUIZ

Should the following sentence use *awhile* or *a while*?

> I haven't heard from you for _____; did I correct your grammar usage too often?

The phrase *for a while* is correct.

{ CHAPTER FOUR }

High Style

Just like with fashion, there's good style and, well, tragic style when it comes to writing. To make sure you're in the former camp, follow these style and usage rules.

75. Order of Adjectives

From the perspective of our hapless English-learning friends around the globe, the order in which we place our adjectives seems completely arbitrary. How is it that a *big red rubber ball* could sound and feel so perfect to a native speaker of English, while a *rubber red big ball* is so comically, tragically wrong?

INCORRECT

- A pulsing *shiny bright tiny* piece of glitter is sparkling on your nose.
- I just bought *handmade brown two acoustic expensive classical beautiful* guitars.

CORRECT

As languages evolve over time, they develop certain conventions that serve as the norm for their speakers. Native English speakers often just *know* when something sounds wrong, even if they may not know that they're adhering to a rule—in this situation, a rule about the order of adjectives—and they can't name it. In English, adjectives appear in the following order: quantity (*one*), quality (*good*), size (*small*), age (*new*), shape (*square*), color (*cobalt*), origin (*Austrian*), material (*bamboo*), and qualifier (*borrowed*) plus noun (*jewelry box*). You have *one good small new square cobalt Austrian bamboo borrowed* jewelry box. Even if we remove half of these categories, they appear in the same order: It's a *small square bamboo* jewelry box.

MORE TO KNOW

If you use more than three or four adjectives, your readers will likely roll their eyes at your purple prose. Of all the stealthy, bizarre rules to innately understand in one's native language, this has to be one of the most arcane.

76. Further vs. Farther

When considering *further* and *further*, it is easy to imagine the toiling writer slowing down, thinking carefully, and using the wrong word. Is it *farther* or *further*? Should I give up and reframe my sentence?

INCORRECT

- We need to walk about two miles *further* to get to the ice cream factory.
- You should *farther* explore the wisdom of wearing a clown nose to an interview.
- They'll need to get gas in the car if they want to drive any *further*.

CORRECT

Farther is about physical distance. How *far* can you drive? How much *farther* can you drive? If you want to walk any *farther* to get to the ice cream factory, I'm going to hitch a ride.

The metaphorical use of "farther down the road" to mean "in the future" retains that sense of distance. *Further* refers to the idea of going more fully into an issue: examining it *further*.

MORE TO KNOW

Further takes you deep into the weeds of exploration and discovery. If you discuss something *further*, you ponder its origins, trajectory, and deeper implications. Derived from Old English, it means "to a greater extent" rather than a physical distance traveled. It also functions as a verb: to *further* one's goals. Oddly enough, *further* and *farther* were not historically separated in meaning.

QUIZ

Should you end the following sentence with *further* or *farther*?

> I refuse to discuss this grammatical matter any _____.

If you refuse to discuss this matter any *further*, it means that you no longer wish to explore it in any detail.

77. Accept vs. Except

If you drive through a parking lot in an average American city, you'll see signs pointing to places where you may or may not park. A sign may read, "No Parking Except Employees," meaning only employees may park there. *Accept and except* sound similar when spoken aloud, but they have opposite meanings.

INCORRECT

- Why did my students refuse to *except* my suggestions?
- I love chocolates, *accept* the ones with cherries inside.
- I am honored to *except* the job of being a teacher.

CORRECT

To *accept* means to receive or acknowledge, while *except* means to remove, exclude, or disallow. Students refuse to *accept* (receive) suggestions when they are worded poorly. I really do love chocolate, *except* (excluding) the ones with cherries; they have a cloying taste, so I won't eat them. I *accepted* the job of being a teacher, and it is an honor to do this work.

MORE TO KNOW

Both *accept* ("take something to oneself") and *except* ("take out") are rooted in Latin; notice, however, that *accept* describes an act of taking in and *except* describes an act of taking out. Any one of us can *accept* (take in) a number of criticisms, *except* (take out) the mean-spirited ones.

78. Redundancies

We have all clawed our way through the weeds of redundancy: *at this point in time, past history, final ending, burning hot fire,* and many more. The only thing they do is stall getting to the point. They do not make one's writing more descriptive, graceful, or elegant.

INCORRECT

- I was a concise writer until *that point in time.*
- He paid for that bouncy house with *cash money.*
- They *quickly* ran as *fast* as they could.

CORRECT

It is no surprise that water is wet, for example, so why saddle your prose with that redundancy? Instead, use your words to convey the characteristic of its wetness rather than to repeat that it is wet: Water can ooze, splash, drip, pour, and cascade right off the page in your readers' minds. You needn't write "unexpected surprise" because all surprises are unexpected, and "pretenses" don't need to be identified as "false." Pay for that bouncy house in cash.

MORE TO KNOW

This type of redundancy is called a *pleonasm,* which means "the use of more words than necessary." Common in academia and business alike, pleonasms offer the illusion of clarification without actually clarifying anything. A redundancy simply takes up space rather than adding elegance.

QUIZ

How can you make this sentence more concise?

> At that point in time, I trimmed the fat from the beef in preparation for the big feast.

I trimmed the beef in preparation for the feast.

79. Clichés

Teachers and professors would do a face-palm if the first sentence they encountered in a paper mentioned either *as old as the hills* or *since the dawn of time*. A cliché can be mildly entertaining, as in *a face only a mother could love* or *economical with the truth*, but don't overuse them.

INCORRECT

- I'll *shuffle off this mortal coil* when I'm good and ready.
- You want a new car? We are *poor as church mice*.
- I hope you recognize that *his elevator doesn't go to the top floor*.

CORRECT

Most clichés are folkloric sayings from occupations (*all hands on deck*), sports (*take one for the team*), religions (*robbing Peter to pay Paul*), famous writings such as Shakespearean plays (*pure as the driven snow*), popular culture (*signed, sealed, delivered*), and much more. They express a very specific set of values and reflect exclusive insider knowledge, and are impenetrable to long-suffering English-language learners. Clichés comprise a large proportion of some people's storehouse of phrases; at best, they add color and whimsy to one's writing, but overuse results in stale and uninteresting prose.

MORE TO KNOW

The word *cliché* refers to a block of text used by printers; when they placed a block of text into place, it clicked: in French, *cliché*. Because each of these phrases occurs in a block, they can be clicked into place like *a moveable feast*. Luckily, they can be removed just as easily. To rewrite a cliché, consider getting to the heart of the basic idea, rather than relying on something that has been written too many times already. You have surely heard the expression, *to cut the mustard*. Why not say that someone is easily able to rise to the challenge? A *diamond in the rough* is about great potential; if you wish to convey the quality of a diamond, think about the essential nature of that "diamond" and celebrate it.

Clichés to Avoid Like the Plague

- *all in a day's work*
- *all over the map*
- *as old as the hills*
- *at the end of the day*
- *back to square one*
- *best thing since sliced bread*
- *between a rock and a hard place*
- *by the skin of one's teeth*
- *cut the mustard*
- *deer in the headlights*
- *diamond in the rough*
- *everything but the kitchen sink*
- *face only a mother could love*
- *fit as a fiddle*
- *flash in the pan*
- *fly in the ointment*
- *give the shirt off (one's) back*
- *it is what it is*
- *it's not over till it's over*
- *kick the bucket*
- *knee high to a grasshopper*

- *let the cat out of the bag*
- *only time will tell*
- *pass with flying colors*
- *play your cards right*
- *run it up the flagpole*
- *since the dawn of time*
- *snowball's chance in hell*
- *take the bull by the horns*
- *vanished into thin air*
- *when pigs fly*
- *the whole enchilada*
- *the writing is on the wall*

80. Jargon

Jargon is directed toward insiders; it is similar to cliché in that one needs insider knowledge to understand it, and much of it is quite bad. Academics use *epistemology*, *ontology*, and *alterity*; businesses use *think outside the box* and *land and expand*; and police officers use *code four*, *perp walk*, and *copy*. And that isn't all!

INCORRECT

- Folks, we need to *shift a paradigm* and locate our *core competency*.
- If we fully understood their *epistemology*, we could *access* their knowledge.
- They need to *up their game* by *actionizing* their accounts.

CORRECT

Jargon is both a form of insider-based shorthand and a way to avoid a more detailed explanation. It can be in the form of eyebrow-raising imagery (trying to *get your ducks in a row* or *move the needle*), and if it's causing you confusion, it immediately tells you that you are not part of that particular insider group. It also supports the tendency to turn nouns into verbs, such as *access* and *impact*. Be daring! Dare to speak more simply, and with a bit of originality. Don't *up your game*; strive to do a better job.

FUN FACT

If jargon sounds like birds chattering meaninglessly to you, then you come by that impression honestly. The word is rooted in Old French and means "a chattering of birds." It went downhill from there—most of us like birds, after all—to mean idle, unintelligible nonsense.

81. Singular "They"

Native English speakers use the singular *they* all the time in conversation. For example, you might hear this: "Ooh, someone left a cookie; I hope *they* don't mind if I eat it." Similarly, you might notice sentences such as "Should each professor do *their* own grading?" This is normal speech, and normal—casual—writing, but is it correct?

INCORRECT

- Every student needs to pick up *his or her* essay so *he or she* can correct it.
- This is *his or her* coat; did *he or she* leave already? We should tell *him or her*.
- Every time I lecture, at least one person is always on *his* cellphone.

CORRECT

We live in a time when writing "he/she," "he or she," and "s/he" has become increasingly awkward and cumbersome. Saying "Did *they* leave already?" to refer to an unknown person is fine; that's how we already speak. As we collectively transition toward more gender-neutral writing, dictionaries and grammar guides are slowly adopting this usage. *The Chicago Manual of Style* recommends avoiding singular *they* in formal writing, but now offers guidance for its use with someone who doesn't identify with a gender-specific pronoun. If you are writing for a publication that relies on a specific style guide, investigate that style guide's advice.

MORE TO KNOW

Singular *they* was already in place by the 1300s; it became "incorrect" only about 600 years later. Similarly, the use of *he* to refer to every individual, male or female, occurred by the late 1800s and is totally inappropriate. Because we are actively modifying the usage of this pronoun, formal writers can simply pluralize the noun until *every* grammar guide allows the singular *they*: Students need to pick up *their* essays.

82. Differences Between American English and British English

Both American English and British English are correct in their own distinct locations, but things fall apart when you place an English person in an American context, or an American person in a British context. Just to tease our British friends, let us assume in this entry that British English is wrong, wrong, wrong in America!

INCORRECT

- His *neighbour's behaviour* was *coloured* by his indifferent approach to *labour*.
- My British friend sent her adult child to *gaol* in an attempt to *civilise* her.
- I certainly *learnt* my lesson when I arrived late to the *theatre*.

CORRECT

Leaving aside our mutually unintelligible slang words and phrases, the biggest difference between our two nations, "separated by a common language," is spelling. Between *learned/learnt, center/centre, traveled/travelled, civilize/civilise,* and others, the differences are minor. Many Americans still use *theatre* because it seems to look more refined (and they will defend their choice with fervor), but keep in mind that Shakespeare himself purportedly used *theater*.

MORE TO KNOW

We can blame Noah Webster, a lexicographer and the creator of *An American Dictionary of the English Language* (1828), for many alterations to British spelling. He wanted to rid English of any "corruptions" from French (which included –re rather than –er). Our collective perception of class differences through the British use of *needn't, shall,* and *shan't,* and the American use of *gotten, pants,* and *cookies* keeps us on our toes.

83. Contranyms

Words with two opposing meanings make no sense, but they exist. How can you possibly convey what you mean when you want someone to "dust the cake"? Should you use a dusting brush over it, potentially messing up the frosting, or should you dust sprinkles all over it, gilding the lily?

INCORRECT

- I guess when you *overlooked* the garden, you *overlooked* the missing violets.
- Be careful to *screen* the living room windows before you *screen* the film.

CORRECT

Contranyms, also known as Janus words, have two opposite meanings, both of which are equally valid. To *dust* is "to cover with particles" and "to remove particles." To *sanction* is "to support" and "to condemn." To *trim* means "to cut something away" and "to decorate with something." Confusion may reign when you *skip* while *skipping* class. Avoid using a contranym twice in the same sentence.

FUN FACT

Janus was the guardian of thresholds; a quick image search for him will reveal two faces looking in opposite directions. Connected to the in-between times and places of doorways, changes, and beginnings, Janus is one source of our transitional month January (the other is Juno). Because the name is old, it diversified. It is also connected to janitor, the person who oversees the transition from dirty to clean.

84. Gendered Professions

Have you heard of a "lady plumber" or a "woman writer" (or any other profession)? How about "gentleman plumber" or "man writer" (or any other profession)? What's wrong with this picture?

INCORRECT

- Wow! I went to class and my teacher is a *man professor*!
- A *lady auto mechanic* worked on my car.
- My daughter is a *woman doctor*.

CORRECT

Job titles and professions are increasingly neutral when it comes to the sex of the person doing the work. The job of a plumber, nurse, pilot, or caregiver can belong to anyone. The error in the examples is in using *lady*, *woman*, *gentleman*, or *man* rather than *female* and *male*. You might have a female mechanic and a male nurse, and no one would think twice. But because gendering professions doesn't make sense, why not just call them writers, plumbers, nurses, pilots, and caregivers?

MORE TO KNOW

Lady, woman, gentleman, and *man* are all nouns. In assigning an individual to a profession, the noun of the profession (e.g., *plumber*) needs an adjective (e.g., *female*), not a noun (e.g., *woman*), if one *must* indicate it. This tendency to gender professions is likely to disappear in the next decade or so.

85. Religions and Their Adherents

Nothing is awkward about religions or those who practice them. The only awkward bit is that those of us who write about them sometimes cannot seem to keep the differences straight between the religion itself (*Judaism*, for example) and the religious practitioners (*Jews*).

INCORRECT

- My neighbors are *Islams*; our children go to school together.
- I had forgotten that your aunt was a devout follower of *Catholic*.
- Your surname is Bhattacharya? Isn't that a *Hinduism* name?

CORRECT

Any map of world religions will reveal about a dozen different colors across the globe, representing variants of Buddhism, Hinduism, Christianity, Islam, Judaism, and others. Buddhists practice Buddhism, Hindus practice Hinduism, Christians practice Christianity, Catholics practice Catholicism, Muslims practice Islam, and Jews practice Judaism. Each major religion includes multiple variants as well as individual branches; that is the norm. Our job is to differentiate between the religion and the practitioner. Your neighbors are *Muslims* who practice *Islam*. Bhattacharya is a *Hindu* name.

MORE TO KNOW

Although this is not specifically an issue of grammar, it is common to link a religion with both its practitioners and a specific place. It is best to separate them. Not all Arabs are Muslims; Arab Christians and Arab Jews also live in the Arab world. Not all Jews are Israelis, and not all Christians are Middle Easterners. Believers span the globe, and nonbelievers live in places with some of the most devout followers.

86. Writing Numbers

You may be asking yourself, this book is supposed to be about words, not numbers, right? And yet, as much as some of us may wish to avoid them, we still need to deal with numbers occasionally in writing. And they come with their own set of rules. Because we speak about numbers easily and with confidence—for example, noting three goldfinches at the backyard feeder—it serves our writing well to be able to get those numbers into the appropriate print form.

INCORRECT

- *15* people took selfies last year in dangerous situations.
- Our colleagues have worked here for *two*, *5*, and *twelve* years, respectively.
- I like *three fourth's* of his songs.

CORRECT

Always spell out numbers at the beginning of sentences: "*Fifteen* people took selfies." When you have a list of numbers, be consistent regardless of how many each one indicates: "for *two*, *five*, and *twelve* years" is consistent. When it comes to writing fractions, hyphenate when spelled out, but do not use an apostrophe: "I like *three-fourths* of his songs."

MORE TO KNOW

Ordinal numbers tell the order of things (*first*, *second*, *third*, etc.), whereas cardinal numbers count: *one*, *two*, *three*, and beyond. Few people actually write out sentences such as "This is the *twenty-six thousandth* time I have told you." We might say these words, but we rarely write them. Instead, we usually write sentences such as "I have told you *26,000* times."

87. "Verbing" and "Nouning"

Bill Watterson (the creator of the comic strip *Calvin and Hobbes*, about a boy and his imaginary friend/stuffed tiger) had Calvin say in 1993 that "verbing weirds language." "To verb," in that context, is to turn a noun, such as *picture*, into a verb: *picture*. Sometimes it works. Sometimes it doesn't.

INCORRECT

- You should *glass* your back porch; that way you can *coffee* out there.
- I promise to *calendar* our meeting next time.
- I'm going to *lavender* all the folded sheets so they smell good.

CORRECT

Language is a living thing. We are accustomed to many verbs that once existed solely as nouns: *phone, clutter, access, impact,* and others. If you use social media, you might *friend* someone. It is when these alterations are unfamiliar that they become jarring (or funny, sometimes), as in "Don't forget to pee the dog." To *lavender* the sheets is clear enough; it just sounds wrong. And I won't be *coffeeing* anytime soon, as much as I love coffee.

MORE TO KNOW

The opposite of verbing is nouning, which is when you turn a verb into a noun, with sometimes appalling consequences:

"Let me *calendar* that." It sounds wrong every time I hear it. The unfortunate truth, however, is that most examples of verbing and nouning are only incorrect until the moment they become normal, as in "Was it a nice *drive*?" and "*Picture* our home, right here." Sigh.

88. Comparatives

Because irregular comparatives such as *better, worse, more,* and *less* are quite common, children learn right away not to say *worser* and *gooder*. Any other such wisdom about comparatives slides right out of our minds as soon as we leave grade school, apparently. It is curiouser and curiouser, to quote Lewis Carroll.

INCORRECT

- My dog has become *sedentarier* since he turned fifteen.
- My child is *boreder* in school this year than ever before.

CORRECT

When an adjective has a single syllable, add –r or –er to make it *bluer, wetter, brighter,* etc. When it ends in –y, change the y to –ier, as in *tidier, noisier,* and *creamier*. Depending on the word, you may need to include the word *more* with the original adjectives (and adverbs): *more anxious, more bored, more annoyed*, and [adverb] *more vividly*. With more than two syllables, always use *more*, as in *more slippery*.

MORE TO KNOW

A solecism, such as *curiouser and curiouser*, is a nonstandard expression or a phrase that is not grammatically correct, but which has come into common usage, usually as an entertaining in-crowd reference. Anyone who has been to Hawai'i knows that *mo' bettah* is a phrase many Hawaiians use regularly. Sometimes such turns of phrase become normalized when repeatedly written or spoken by a public figure or author—just sayin'.

89. Superlatives

Comparatives and superlatives live next door to each other in our minds; that must be why we mess them up so often. It is one easy step from *darker* to *darkest* and from *more boring* to *most boring*. We run into trouble when we use the wrong attachment, as with a vacuum cleaner.

INCORRECT

- Thank you for giving me the *finerest* send-off that I could hope for.
- You guys are the *bestest* buddies ever!
- We'll be friends when *worst comes to worst.*

CORRECT

You can form most superlatives by adding –st or –est to the original adjective, as in *finest*, or by adding –iest to an adjective that ends in *y*, as in *happiest*. Just don't do either of those to an irregular word such as *good* or *bad*. *Bestest* is a redundancy because *best* is already the best! And it's when *worse* (comparative) comes to *worst* (superlative) that conditions are difficult.

MORE TO KNOW

Follow the same rules for superlatives as for comparatives when it comes to the number of syllables, as in *roundest, liveliest*, and *most interesting* (using *most* rather than *more*). Note that you need to double the consonant to create *wettest* and *reddest* when the original has a consonant-vowel-consonant spelling, and remove the *y* to make *driest* and *busiest*. Learn these rules and you'll be the *cleverest* writer among all your friends.

90. Feel Good vs. Feel Well

James Brown sang out, "I feel good! I knew that I would." He felt happy, as we all did when we heard him. Because both *good* (adjective, noun, adverb) and *well* (noun, adjective, adverb) serve multiple functions, consider the use of *feel* in order to choose correctly.

INCORRECT

- I have dropped my ice cream on the sidewalk and I *feel badly*.
- His uncle *feels goodly* today; he had some ice cream too.
- You received an A on the exam? Wow, you must *feel well*!

CORRECT

If you *feel good,* like James Brown did, you're in good spirits and on top of your game (and maybe you had some ice cream, too). If you *feel well,* you feel healthy. If you *feel bad,* you are in pain or feel sorry for yourself. If you *feel badly,* however, that means your neurological system is messed up and that you may have become numb! You can *feel bad* over dropping your ice cream; *feeling badly* may have caused you to let go.

MORE TO KNOW

Feel is a linking verb, similar to *look* and *taste*. If you write that the "coffee tastes *good*," it is the coffee itself that has the good flavor, not the coffee that is capable of tasting! Use an adjective (*great, delicious, angry*), not an adverb (*angrily, beautifully, thrillingly*) to describe how you are, feel, taste, look, sound, and smell. James Brown was right! He *feels good.*

91. Parallel Structure

People love making lists, particularly when those lists involve either things to do or things not to do. Woody Guthrie's fine list of "New Years Rulin's" (1943) included 33 commands (available online for your perusal). Each command appears in the imperative tense, including "save dough, change socks, and love everybody." His list uses precise parallel construction, unlike those of nearly all the rest of us.

INCORRECT

- They love writing, dancing, and *to read.*
- I told her to focus, *write well,* and to turn in her essay on time.
- Stop doing these things: playing with your phone and *don't fidget.*

CORRECT

Once you have launched a list, stay consistent. If you love to write, dance, and read, you don't need *to* to set off the last one. If you told her *to* focus, *to* write well, and *to* turn in her essay, keep the parallels. Lastly, when we tell someone what to do and what not to do, we shouldn't mix negatives and positives freely. Oops.

MORE TO KNOW

The reason parallel construction is important has to do with the need to indicate equal importance in a list. If you have ever said "I need *cat litter, food,* and *water,* but not in that order," you recognize that cat litter is fairly far down on the list of things you need to live. If you say "I need *food, water,* and *clothing,*" the parallel structure suggests that each one is important.

QUIZ

Is it necessary to add anything to the following sentence?

> They told us that we should eat, that we should drink, and ___ be merry.

To achieve parallel construction, *that we should* needs to be repeated before *be merry.*

92. Better Than He/Him

English grammar can be at its worst when certain key words are left out. We are accustomed to questions and answers such as "Did you go to the store?" and "I did," because *did* substitutes for the repetition of *went to the store*. But what does one do with "I am better than she"? She *what*? Shouldn't it be *her*?

INCORRECT

- He is a stronger man *than I*.
- Your cousin Brandon is more famous *than we*.
- Are these people better *than they*?

CORRECT

Brandon is more famous than we *what?* Brandon is more famous than us. If we treat *than* as a preposition (such as *above* or *over*), then *me* is the obvious answer. He is stronger *than me*. If we treat *than* as a conjunction (such as *and* or *if*), then *I* works best. She writes better *than I* (do). Note that if you use *I, he, she,* or other subject pronouns, the rest of the sentence will always be implied.

MEMORY TIP

Ask yourself what is implied by the missing words: Is it the verb? If "She writes more letters to Mom *than I*," we assume that she writes more letters to Mom than I do. However, if

"She writes more letters to Mom *than me,*" we know that she writes more to Mom than she writes *to me,* even without *to me* in the sentence.

QUIZ

Should you use *he* or *him* in the following sentence?

> I've spent more time with you than _____.

I've spent more time with you than *him.*

93. Active Voice vs. Passive Voice

The battle for self-expression in American culture is caught between two competing ideologies: to be straightforward and take responsibility, or to be modest and go along for the good of others. These ideologies are mistakenly ascribed to active and passive voice, respectively.

INCORRECT

- The lamp *was broken* by someone who definitely was not me.
- A bold statement *was made* by my cousin's use of the active voice.
- All kinds of new experiments are *being conducted* by scientists.

CORRECT

When we use active voice, American readers automatically and perhaps mistakenly give us more credit for honesty, clarity, and wisdom. When passive voice is used by us, we're said to be unconvincing by our readers. When *the lamp is broken,* we don't know by whom. Make a bold statement; don't let a bold statement be made. Lastly, scientists are the ones conducting experiments, and should appear first in the sentence. Scientists *are conducting* all kinds of new experiments.

MORE TO KNOW

In some languages besides English (such as Indonesian, Swahili, and Japanese), active voice is considered rude, and passive voice is preferred. Appropriate times to use passive voice in English include when you don't know who did it ("This guitar *was built* in 1982"), when who did it doesn't matter ("The trees *were taken down* in the storm"), or when you focus on the action ("The poem *was cited* widely").

94. Number Agreement

We can all agree that I am, you are, and they are all aware of how most sentences should fit together. However, the place many of us collapse is in connecting a subject and its verb in a longer sentence. *We*, of the many childhood grammatical errors, still *go* to school. But we are tempted to write *goes*.

INCORRECT

- It's a good thing *he*, with all his many accolades, *are* settling down.
- Our *friends* have been visiting the Adirondacks their whole *life*.
- The government *are* changing *their* minds daily.

CORRECT

The first two errors have to do with the position of something of a different number right next to the word that agrees with the subject. "*He is* settling down." Don't be fooled by the plural *accolades*; they aren't settling down. "*Our friends have* done this their whole *lives*." Your job is to carefully note the number of the subject—*our friends, he, they, we*, the *neighbors*—and link it to the verb or other words.

MORE TO KNOW

American English treats collective entities (government, band, gang) as singular, while the British treat them as plural: "The Catholic Church *are centred* in the Vatican

City." Beyond that one distinction, however, number agreement means that the subject and the verb must always be linked, no matter how many qualifiers divide them. The *bird* [single] and all of its many feathers, two feet, and two wings, *was* lovely.

QUIZ

Should the following collective entity be considered singular or plural?

> I am going out to hear a band tonight. That band _____ fantastic!

If you are American, that *band is* fantastic! If you are British, that *band are* "not bad."

95. Orient, Orientate, and Oriental

One of these is not like the others! And since language is a living thing, and societies and cultures change, one has fallen into disuse and disfavor.

INCORRECT

- I will be ready in a minute; I just need to *orientate* myself.
- We just returned from the most exotic and mysterious visit to *the Orient*!
- Confucius was one of most influential *Oriental* people.

CORRECT

If *to orient* oneself means "learning one's environment," *to orientate* means to do the same thing in the British-speaking world as a back-formation from *orientation*. They mean the same thing, but each one is "wrong" in the other context. Furthermore, British English differentiates between "Asians" (South Asians) and "Orientals" (East Asians). It is fine to use *oriental* anywhere in the English-speaking world, but with rugs only. If you wish to use *the Orient,* use quotation marks to add a hint of irony. Ha! He longs to go to "the Orient"!

MORE TO KNOW

Oriental refers to the rising sun, which is in the East. Using *of the Orient* assumes a *western* viewpoint, looking eastward. Asians are not "east" from their perspective; they are at home.

QUIZ

What is the best usage of orient and oriental, with or without capitalization?

> I need to_____ myself so that I can figure out where to place my_____ rug.

I need to *orient* myself; the *oriental* rug will look gorgeous regardless.

---

96. Among/Amongst and While/Whilst

We are firmly in the thorny territory of the separation of American English from British English here, along with shifts in usage over time.

INCORRECT

- Would you make me a cup of tea *whilst* you are in the kitchen?
- I hope to plant lavender *amongst* the roses in the garden.
- Don't laugh *whilst* eating; you might choke.

CORRECT

The examples above are "wrong" to American ears. Instead, make me a cup of tea *while* you are in the kitchen and plant your lavender *among* the roses. Americans tend to view *amongst* and *whilst* as charming (or fussy, depending on their outlook) hallmarks of British English. Speakers of British English (and some older Americans in the southern mountains) mostly use them interchangeably. Words such as *amongst*, *whilst*, and *towards* are called *adverbial genitives*; they are genitive-case nouns that function as adverbs. We use *once, always, afterwards, hence,* and others all the time. They are just as old as *thrice* and *thence,* but we use them more often, so they feel normal.

MORE TO KNOW

Languages evolve in fits and starts, depending on word usage by powerful people, as well as in literature. If you read British children's books, the "incorrect" examples of *whilst* and *amongst* seem normal. Even among (ha!) speakers of British English, the use of *among* is far greater than the use of *amongst*. *Amongst* appears to be on its way out.

97. Discourse Markers

So, have you ever wondered whether it's allowable to start a sentence with a meaningless word such as *so, hey, oh, well,* or *umm*? Wonder no more!

INCORRECT

- *And* I never thought I would see you admit to making a spelling mistake.
- *But* you never told me that sentence was incorrect.
- *Or* I could pretend that it never happened.

CORRECT

These words are called *discourse markers,* and local versions of *so, umm,* and *oh* form a part of everyone's vocabulary, all over the world. The incorrect examples above are *not* wrong because they are conjunctions; they are wrong because they don't set apart the following sentence. A discourse marker calls attention to the speaker, prepares the speaker to begin a sentence, and makes the listener look directly at the speaker. In written works, it signifies casual speech, regionalisms, and can substitute for the vocative (direct address) case, as in "*Bill,* come here."

MORE TO KNOW

You know, no single society in the world will ever stop using discourse markers. After all, they serve a powerful social purpose. You see, we would struggle to continue through life without a little preparation at the beginning of each sentence. I mean, as irritating as this paragraph is to read, the irritation comes from reading too many of them in a row. So, did that make sense?

98. Demonstratives

Writers like to assume that readers can read minds. Would you know what I mean if I were to write "Look at this!" or "Look at that!"? You would not know in advance, which is why you would need to investigate. In writing, *this* is not enough, because your readers are one step removed from your viewpoint.

INCORRECT

- I keep showing them *this*, and they don't understand.
- She couldn't believe he was going over *that* again.
- It is because of *these* that our work is never done.

CORRECT

In each case, the words *this, that, these*, and *those* need a clarifying noun. "I keep showing them *this balance sheet*" is quite clear; for all we know, "I keep showing them *this*" could be in reference to a cup of coffee. If he is "going over *that* again," it might be helpful to know that he was asking her, once again, to get married. Be specific, and all will be clear.

MORE TO KNOW

These words are demonstratives; they demonstrate or point something out. When paired with a noun, they become demonstrative adjectives because of their indication of something specific. The difference between "*the* books," "*these* books" (nearby), and "*those* books" (in the distance) is that with the latter two, we know exactly which books are being discussed.

99. Split Infinitives

Any *Star Trek* fan will instantly recognize the phrase "to boldly go where no one has gone before." While its usage has settled into the popular consciousness, recognize that *boldly* splits *to* and *go*, and results in a split infinitive.

INCORRECT

- She wished *to greedily devour* all that was left of the cookies.
- We explored the library *to gladly discover* a favorite new book.
- I picked up the stack of photos *to carefully sort* them.

CORRECT

According to some editors, adverbs are the enemy of good writing. This choice is up to you, of course; should you include adverbs in your work, less is more. In the case of *to greedily devour, devour* already implies greed. When one discovers a favorite new book, gladness is already implied. If you must sort photos, sort them carefully; the adverb appears at the end of the sentence.

MORE TO KNOW

An infinitive is a verb in its unconjugated form; i.e., *to think, to do, to explore*. We use them in sentences paired with other verbs, such as "I *ventured* [verb 1] out in the snow *to shop* [verb 2, infinitive]." When we split that infinitive in two, we place an adverb between the *to* and the verb, as in "I ventured out in the snow *to [brazenly] shop*."

100. Indeterminate Personal Pronoun Usage

Personal pronouns are so useful; we scatter them through our sentences without a second thought. We use them so often that sometimes we forget to specify which noun the pronoun indicates, so that occasionally we might think we're referring to a person baking, but the sentence tells us that it's a cat doing the work.

INCORRECT

- The cat watched Marie while she baked; *she* was working hard.
- Jack knew how happy his father would be once *he* returned home at last.
- I added my phone to the pile of phones; *it* was buzzing with incoming texts.

CORRECT

The vague designations of personal pronouns—*she, he, it, they*—require us to focus attention on the main figure in the sentence. The cat may have been working hard, but *Marie* was doing the baking. If you cannot tell whether Jack or his father was returning home, being more specific will focus attention on Jack's *father*. Whether the phone or the pile of phones was buzzing is a mystery!

MORE TO KNOW

Personal pronouns stand in for nouns. They make sentences flow smoothly, help us avoid repetition, and offer creative possibilities. Consider "Bob knew *he* would need all his wits about him," and "Bob knew Bob would need all Bob's wits about Bob"! By using personal pronouns to indicate the agent or actor in the sentence, you can avoid writing "The dog watched the squirrel; *he* leaped out of danger."

Parts of Speech Cheat Sheet

These nine parts of speech are the building blocks of sentences; knowing them will lower the likelihood of your developing a tragically incorrect sentence.

adjective	describes a noun or pronoun (*lucky, cold, blooming, wary*)	The *fluffy* kitten sought *comforting* attention from its *exhausted* owner.
adverb	modifies an adjective or verb by indicating how, when, or where (*slowly, today, south*)	My mom *clearly* described the event *yesterday* by *slowly* enumerating each part.
article	determines whether a noun is specific (*the*) or nonspecific (*a, an*)	Give me *an* apple so that I can add it to *the* stew with *the* chicken and *the* onions.
conjunction	connects words, phrases, or ideas logically (*and, but, because, or*)	We ate cake *and* ice cream *but* no chocolate sauce *or* whipped cream.

interjection	an exclamation that indicates emotion or urgency (*so, ouch, dude, wow*)	*Oh! Hey!* You forgot your essay.
noun	a person, place, thing, or idea (*goats, a politi-cian, joy, San Francisco*)	*Jim* sat on the *ground* with his *son* to examine *bugs* under the *rock*.
preposition	connects a noun or pronoun to other words (*from, in, above, to*)	Ellie gave the essay *to* me *after* I climbed *onto* the dais *with* my computer.
pronoun	a word that substitutes for a noun or noun phrase (*he, yours, they, her*)	*They* realized *their* mistake immediately when *their* professor narrowed *his* eyes.
verb	an action word in all its forms (*went, sigh, laugh, woop, crawl*)	I *finished* my essay, then I *leaped* onto the bar and *celebrated*!

Here are all the parts of a sentence, indicated one by one:

She *[pronoun]* saw *[verb]* the *[article]* extent *[noun]* of *[preposition]* the *[article]* errors *[noun]* in *[preposition]* John's *[noun]* writing *[noun]*, and *[conjunction]* immediately *[adverb]* chose *[verb]* not *[negation]* to *[preposition]* date *[verb]* him *[pronoun]*. Wow! *[interjection]*

Punctuation Cheat Sheet

’ apostrophe	used for possessives, contractions, and some holidays	*Andy’s piano didn’t arrive in time for Mother’s Day.*
: colon	used to introduce a list, to separate two clauses, and as a symbol in math or time	*Here is what you need to buy: milk, bread, eggs, and a puppy.*
, comma	used at the points where one might breathe if reading aloud, or to separate items	*Tragically, his grammatical ambitions did not match his capabilities.*
– — dashes	em dashes replace parentheses, a pair of commas, and a colon; en dashes connect numbers and ideas	*On Tuesday (2–3 p.m.) I’ll focus on one thing—chocolate.*
. . . ellipsis	used to indicate that something has been left out of a sentence or phrase, or the trailing off of a thought. . .	*If I had intended to take out the . . . garbage, I would have done it already.*

Mark	Use	Example
! exclamation point	used to indicate something surprising or in need of emphasis	*Wow! You wrote a perfect essay! Congratulations!*
- hyphen	used to join adjectives before a noun, attach a prefix, clarify pronunciation, indicate fractions, join compound numbers, and many other uses	*The students' half-baked attempt to comply with my ten-second tirade resulted in just three-fourths of the class appearing before the pre-eminent scholar.*
( ) parentheses	used to include more information, aside from the main point	*If you had asked me (and I was hoping you would), I might have made us some tea.*
. period	used to end a sentence, and with some abbreviations	*I need you to persuade him to use proper grammar. He has a job interview at 10 a.m.*
? question mark	used to indicate a question	*Why does she keep leaving her coffee cup in the sink?*

“ ” quotation marks	used to indicate direct speech, phrases, or quoted material. Note: When quotation marks are used within quotation marks, a single quotation mark is used, as in the example to the right.	*"He said 'Tuesday afternoon' when I asked about his arrival time."*
; semicolon	used to separate two independent clauses that are related	*My office has a nice window; it looks out into the forest.*

50 Substitutions for Long-Winded Phrases

While purple prose might well have pleased a grandmother of the nineteenth century, being concise today frees you to focus on what matters: the point.

✖	✔
adequate number of	enough
an estimated	about
arrived at an agreement	agreed
as a result of	because
as the means by which	to
assuming that	if

✖	✔
at this point in time	now
back in the day	[at least name the decade]
be in a position to	can
call a halt to	stop
come to an agreement	agree
despite the fact that	despite
due to the fact that	because
during the period of	during
for the sum of	for
has the capability of	can
inasmuch as	because
in a timely manner	soon
in close proximity	near

✖	in advance of	✔	before
✖	in connection with	✔	with
✖	in light of the fact that	✔	because
✖	in many cases	✔	often
✖	in order that	✔	so
✖	in reference to	✔	about
✖	in spite of the fact that	✔	even though
✖	in terms of	✔	regarding
✖	in the amount of	✔	for
✖	in the course of	✔	during
✖	in the near future	✔	soon
✖	in the possession of	✔	has

✖	✔
in the unlikely event of	if
in this day and age	today
in view of the fact that	because
it is essential that	must
it is incumbent upon	must
it is very likely that	probably
it would appear that	apparently
make a determination	decide
not in a position to	can't
notwithstanding the fact that	although
of the opinion that	believe
perform an assessment of	assess

✖	✔
pertaining to	about
provides guidance for	guides
subsequent to	after
sufficient quantities	enough
until such time as	until
with regard to	about
with the exception of	except for

Glossary

adjective: a descriptive word that modifies a noun, as in *beautiful, lively, funny, large,* and *red.*

American English: the type of English spoken by people of the United States and, sometimes, Canada (but usually only when they have been influenced by American popular culture).

British English: the type of English spoken by people of the United Kingdom and most of its former colonies: England, Scotland, Wales, Ireland, India, Nigeria, Canada, Australia, New Zealand, and dozens of islands and territories. The exception is the United States.

clause: a phrase that contains a verb, as in "*We were going to the ballpark.*" A main clause forms a complete sentence, as in "*We took him with us.*" A dependent clause is incomplete, as in "*because he couldn't stay home alone.*" The dependent clause can attach to the main clause.

comparative: adjectives that compare two things, such as *wetter, crazier,* and *more content.*

conjunction: words that join phrases, including *for, and, nor, but, or, yet,* and *so*. FANBOYS is an easy-to-remember mnemonic for them.

consonant: a letter in the alphabet that creates a specific closed sound, such as *d, t,* or *m*. English has 21 consonants.

contraction: a word in which two letters, such as *nt,* are joined by an apostrophe to indicate that there is a missing letter or letters between them. For example, *can't* = *cannot.*

diacritical marks: accent marks such as *á, ñ,* and *ö.*

etymology: the study of word origins.

genitive: the indication that one noun is related to another, as in *the cat's meow* and *the meow of the cat.*

gerund: an –ing verb that functions as a noun, as in "*Cooking* is a special joy for me."

grammar: the system of rules and practices that govern the way a language works.

homophone: words that sound the same but are different in meaning, spelling, or origins.

idiom: a word or phrase that indicates something different from the actual words, as in "My brother is *sawing logs* in his room."

interjection: a word or phrase that serves as an aside or to convey emotion, as in *no way, whoa, oy,* or *dang.*

intransitive: an action word that does not need an object, such as *"I sat"* or *"They read"*; see also: transitive.

irregular verb: a verb that does not follow conventional forms such as "I laugh," "He laughs," and "You laughed." Instead, an irregular verb might read, *"I go," "He goes,"* and *"You went."*

modal verbs: a verb that indicates possibility or necessity, as in *could, must,* or *might.*

modifier: an adjective or noun that changes the main noun, such as *good-looking* man.

nominative: a noun or pronoun that serves as the subject of a verb, as in "*We* went."

noun phrase: two or more words that modify a noun, such as "*my new* pen," "the woman *who stole yard signs,"* and "the competition *to win.*"

object: the part of the sentence being acted upon by the subject, as in "The dog ate *my homework.*"

parallel construction: using the same form of repetition within a sentence, as in "He ate *two eggs, two waffles,* and *three strawberries."*

participle: a past (–ed) or present (–ing) form of a verb that can be used as an adjective (the *howling* wind), a noun (*photo-*

graphing animals is great), or part of a multipart verb when used with an auxiliary or helping verb (*was eating* or *had been*).

phrasal verb: a context-specific idiomatic phrase, such as *break down*, comprising a verb or adverb + a preposition. It usually means something different from its literal interpretation.

plural: a noun or verb that indicates more than one person or thing, as in "three *chairs*."

possessive: when one wishes to indicate ownership or relationship, as in "He is *my* dog."

predicate: the part of a sentence that includes the verb, as in "He [subject] *went to the store* [predicate]."

prose: one or more sentences written without attention paid to meter, such as the one you're reading right now. Poetry in strict metric format, such as a sonnet, is the opposite of prose.

punctuation: a range of symbols that illustrate how sentences divide, and that help clarify meaning. For example, "Let's eat, Grandma" differs from "Let's eat Grandma."

quotation marks: a type of punctuation (") that indicates quoted material or a word used in irony.

relative pronoun: words such as *that*, *which*, *who*, and *when*; they connect a clause that relates to the main part of the sentence. For example, "I ate food *that* I brought to work."

root: a word from which other words can be constructed, as in *spire* leading to *aspire, perspire, respire, conspire,* and others.

singular: a noun or verb that refers to just one person or thing, as opposed to more than one.

subject: a noun that is doing the acting in a sentence, as in "*Emma* ate lunch."

subjunctive: a way of expressing oneself that indicates something that might happen, as in "*If I were* to have coffee with you, we would probably enjoy ourselves."

superlative: the most extreme form of an adjective, positive or negative, such as *wettest.*

syllable: a syllable is a pronounced unit of a word. Requiring at least one vowel and usually including consonants, a syllable can form a complete word, such as *bat. Battle* is a two-syllable word.

tense: an expression of a verb that indicates time or duration, as in past tense used to describe the word *sat,* or future tense to describe the words *will sit.*

transitive: an action word + the object connected to the action: "He [subject] *brings* [transitive verb] chocolate [object]."

vocative: a word or phrase that points to the person or thing being addressed, as in "*My friend,* you are looking well."

voice: the way we arrange a sentence so that it is active ("*I broke* the lamp") or passive ("The lamp *was broken by me*").

vowel: a letter such as *a*, *e*, *i*, *o*, or *u* that represents one of the many sounds we make; the letter y is a semi-vowel. A vowel is the core of a syllable and is in contrast to the consonant.

Resources

Dictionaries

Everyone needs access to a first-rate dictionary and thesaurus. Fortunately, the online world abounds with such resources. In addition to the ability to browse for words and find definitions and synonyms, **Dictionary.com** (paired with **Thesaurus.com**) has sections on grammar, weird words, history, pop culture, and other features. **Merriam-Webster.com** is another favorite site, with quizzes, words of the day, trending words, and videos. They are often quite responsive to political and social currents, and have a lively social media presence. If exploring word origins is your thing, the Online Etymology Dictionary (**EtymOnline.com**) is excellent when you want to spend an hour going down yet another wonderful rabbit hole.

Online Writing Tools

The Purdue University Online Writing Lab (**OWL.English.Purdue.edu/OWL**) is the preferred free resource tool for professors and students at all levels. The UCLA Graduate Writing Center (**GWC.GSRC.UCLA.edu/Resources**) has compiled some of the best writing tips online and in print, and is well worth exploring. Unlike many other resources, it has sections on writing for specific fields. **Grammarist.com** is quite handy for online grammar questions; the explanations of idiomatic phrases are fascinating.

Books

Barrett, Grant. *Perfect English Grammar: The Indispensable Guide to Excellent Writing and Speaking*. Berkeley, CA: Zephyros Press, 2016.

Written in a welcoming, engaging style, its sections are neatly divided and numbered, making it an easy-to-use handbook. Thanks to its small size, it fits equally well in a bag or on your desk.

Chicago Manual of Style (17th ed.). Chicago: University of Chicago Press, 2017.

This is the gold standard for virtually every question on issues of writing, grammar, citation, and style.

Shapiro, Fred. *The Yale Book of Quotations*. New Haven, CT: Yale University Press, 2006.

This book replaced my well-worn *Bartlett's Familiar Quotations* almost immediately because of its successful sleuthing into original sources. Ask "Who originally said that?" no more!

Williams, J. and Bizup, J. *Style: Lessons in Clarity and Grace* (12th ed.). Chicago: University of Chicago Press, 2016.

This no-nonsense guide to improving your writing goes well beyond grammar and into the elegant world of wielding words, phrases, and sentences with power.

About the Author

SEAN WILLIAMS teaches ethnomusicology, cultural studies, and writing at The Evergreen State College in Olympia, Washington. The author or editor of multiple books, including the award-winning *Bright Star of the West: Joe Heaney, Irish Song Man*, and *The Ethnomusicologists' Cookbook (Volumes 1 and 2)*, she plays over 30 musical instruments (some of them well!). Her social media alter ego, Captain Grammar Pants, provides a daily dose of brightness for those assailed by the (tragically) grammatically incorrect comments of their families and friends.